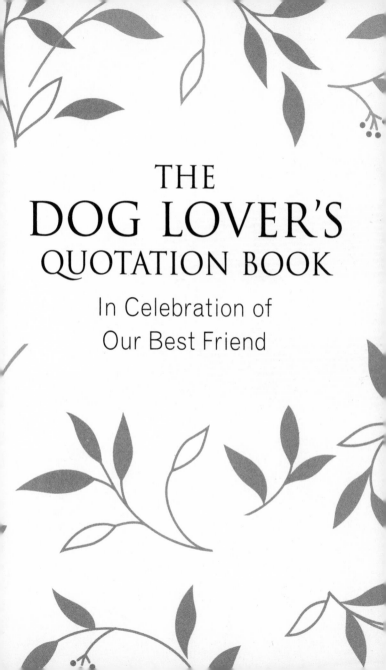

# THE
# DOG LOVER'S
## QUOTATION BOOK

In Celebration of
Our Best Friend

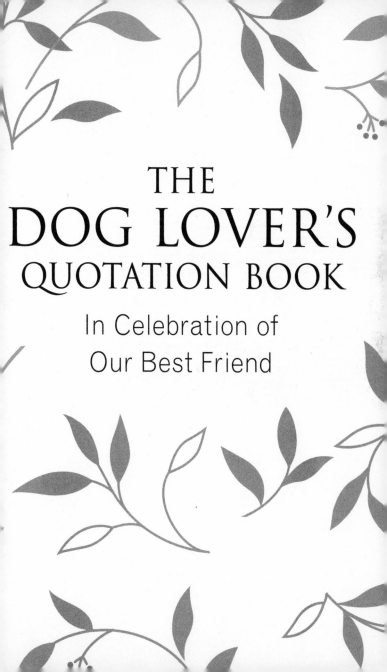

# THE
# DOG LOVER'S
## QUOTATION BOOK

### In Celebration of
### Our Best Friend

*The Dog Lover's Quotation Book*

Text Copyright © 2016 Hatherleigh Press

Library of Congress Cataloging-in-Publication Data is available.

ISBN: 978-1-57826-624-1

Printed in the United States

10 9 8 7 6 5 4 3 2

# CONTENTS

H ER EYES met mine as she walked down the corridor peering apprehensively into the kennels. I felt her need instantly and knew I had to help her.

I wagged my tail, not too exuberantly, so she wouldn't be afraid. As she stopped at my kennel I blocked her view from a little accident I had in the back of my cage. I didn't want her to know that I hadn't been walked today. Sometimes the overworked shelter keepers get too busy and I didn't want her to think poorly of them.

As she read my kennel card I hoped that she wouldn't feel sad about my past. I only have the future to look forward to and want to make a difference in some-one's life.

She got down on her knees and made little kissy sounds at me. I shoved my shoulder and side of my head up against the bars to comfort her. Gentle fingertips caressed my neck; she was desperate for companionship. A tear fell down her cheek and I raised my paw to assure her that all would be well.

Soon my kennel door opened and her smile was so bright that I instantly jumped into her arms.

I would promise to keep her safe.

I would promise to always be by her side.

I would promise to do everything I could to see that radiant smile and sparkle in her eyes.

I was so fortunate that she came down my corridor. So many more are out there

who haven't walked the corridors. So many
more to be saved. At least I could save one.
   I rescued a human today.

—JANINE ALLEN,
   "I Rescued a Human Today"

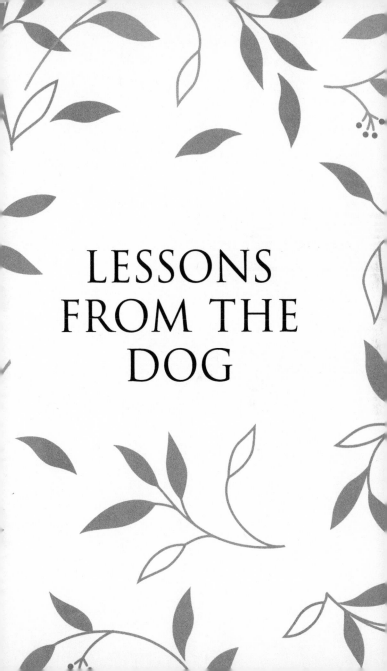

# LESSONS FROM THE DOG

The dogs in our lives, the dogs we come to love and who (we fervently believe) love us in return, offer more than fidelity, consolation, and companionship...They offer, if we are wise enough or simple enough to take it, a model for what it means to give your heart with little thought of return... Perhaps it is not too late for them to teach us some new tricks.

MARJORIE GARBER

We try to teach our dogs new tricks when there's so much we can learn from them.

ROBERT COANE

A person can learn a lot from a dog, even a loopy one like ours. Marley taught me about living each day with unbridled exuberance and joy, about seizing the moment and following your heart. He taught me to appreciate the simple things—a walk in the woods, a fresh snowfall, a nap in a shaft of winter sunlight. And as he grew old and achy, he taught me about optimism in the face of adversity. Mostly, he taught me about friendship and selflessness and, above all else, unwavering loyalty.

JOHN GROGAN

We derive immeasurable good, uncounted pleasures, enormous security, and many critical lessons about life by owning dogs.

ROGER CARAS

Dogs are how people would be if the important stuff is all that mattered to us.

ASHLY LORENZANA

To err is human, to forgive, canine.

AUTHOR UNKNOWN

The dog of your boyhood teaches you a great deal about friendship, and love, and death: Old Skip was my brother. They had buried him under our elm tree, they said—yet this wasn't totally true. For he really lay buried in my heart.

WILLIE MORRIS

If your dog doesn't like someone, you probably shouldn't either.

AUTHOR UNKNOWN

If your dog thinks you're the greatest person in the world, don't seek a second opinion.

JIM FIEBIG

If I could be half the person my dog is, I'd be twice the human I am.

CHARLES YU

Everything I know, I learned from dogs.

NORA ROBERTS

Gratitude: that quality which the Canine Mongrel seldom lacks; which the Human Mongrel seldom possesses!

LION P.S. REES

A boy can learn a lot from a dog: obedience, loyalty, and the importance of turning around three times before lying down.

ROBERT BENCHLEY

Lots of people talk to animals. Not very many listen, though... That's the problem.

BENJAMIN HOFF

God, give me by Your grace what You give
to dogs by nature.

MECHTILDA OF MAGDEBERG

In a world of hypocrisy and betrayal, dogs
are direct. They never lie.

ERICA JONG

It's not the size of the dog in the fight, it's
the size of the fight in the dog.

MARK TWAIN

They [dogs] never talk about themselves but listen to you while you talk about yourself, and keep up an appearance of being interested in the conversation.

JEROME K. JEROME

My dogs forgive anger in me, the arrogance in me, the brute in me. They forgive everything I do before I forgive myself.

GUY DE LA VALDENE

A dog is not considered a good dog because he is a good barker. A man is not considered a good man because he is a good talker.

CHUANG-TZU

I think we are drawn to dogs because they are the uninhibited creatures we might be if we weren't certain we knew better. They fight for honor at the first challenge, make love with no moral restraint, and they do not for all their marvelous instincts appear to know about death. Being such wonderfully uncomplicated beings, they need us to do their worrying.

GEORGE BIRD EVANS

For it is by muteness that a dog becomes for one so utterly beyond value; with him one is at peace, where words play no torturing tricks.

JOHN GALSWORTHY

The reason a dog has so many friends is that he wags his tail instead of his tongue.

AUTHOR UNKNOWN

Many who have spent a lifetime in it can tell us less of love than the child that lost a dog yesterday.

THORNTON WILDER

No animal I know of can consistently be more of a friend and companion than a dog.

STANLEY LEINWOLL

Dogs. They are better than human beings because they know but they do not tell.

EMILY DICKINSON

Dogs are wise. They crawl away into a quiet corner and lick their wounds and do not rejoin the world until they are whole once more.

AGATHA CHRISTIE

My dog does have his failings, of course. He's afraid of firecrackers and hides in the clothes closet whenever we run the vacuum cleaner, but, unlike me he's not afraid of what other people think of him or anxious about his public image.

GARY KOWALSKI

One dog barks at something, the rest bark at him.

CHINESE PROVERB

Dogs come into our lives to teach us about love. They depart to teach us about loss. New dogs can never replace a former one— they merely expand the heart. If you have loved many dogs, your heart is very big.

AUTHOR UNKNOWN

Does not the gratitude of the dog put to shame any man who is ungrateful to his benefactors?

SAINT BASIL

If you pick up a starving dog and make him prosperous, he will not bite you. It is the principal difference between a dog and a man.

MARK TWAIN

They [dogs] motivate us to play, be affectionate, seek adventure and be loyal.

TOM HAYDEN

The world would be a nicer place if everyone had the ability to love as unconditionally as a dog.

M.K. CLINTON

# PUPPY
# LOVE

Happiness is a warm puppy.

CHARLES M. SCHULZ

Every once in a while a puppy enters your life and changes everything.

AUTHOR UNKNOWN

Did you know that there are over 300 words for love in canine?

GABRIELLE ZEVIN

A pup does not know words. It just hears love.

PAMELA DUGDALE

When a puppy wags its tail and barks at the same time, how do you know which end to believe?

AUTHOR UNKNOWN

The greatest love is a mother's; then a dog's; then a sweetheart's.

POLISH PROVERB

A dog may be man's best friend, but a child's best friend is a puppy.

AUTHOR UNKNOWN

When you feel lousy, puppy therapy is indicated.

SARA PARETSKY

No symphony orchestra ever played music like a two-year-old girl laughing with a puppy.

BERN WILLIAMS

When an eighty-five pound mammal licks your tears away, then tries to sit on your lap, it's hard to feel sad.

KRISTAN HIGGINS

If puppies could talk, I would never try to make human friends again.

AUTHOR UNKNOWN

Dogs don't rationalize. They don't hold anything against a person. They don't see the outside of a human but the inside of a human.

CESAR MILLAN

Hold puppies, kittens, and babies anytime you get the chance.

H. JACKSON BROWN, Jr.

Inside every Newfoundland, Boxer, Elkhound and Great Dane is a puppy longing to climb on to your lap.

HELEN THOMSON

Even though it will stumble every step of the way, your puppy will walk towards you to snuggle at your feet.

Even though it hardly has any strength, your puppy will wag its tail to greet you lovingly.

Even though it can barely twist, your puppy will lift its head and look at you adoringly with those cute big eyes.

Even though it is tiny and small, your puppy will think of itself as a lion when it comes to protecting you.

AUTHOR UNKNOWN

It's impossible to keep a straight face in the presence of one or more puppies.

AUTHOR UNKNOWN

Of all the things I miss from veterinary practice, puppy breath is one of the fondest memories!

DR. TOM CAT

Oh the saddest of sights in a world of sin, is the little lost pup with his tail tucked in.

ARTHUR GUITERMAN

Learn from the puppies: Don't clutter where you live.

JAMES L. PAPANDREA

Puppies are nature's remedy for feeling unloved...plus numerous other ailments of life.

RICHARD ALLEN PALM

A puppy is but a dog, plus high spirits, and minus common sense.

AGNES REPPLIER

Puppies are constantly inventing new ways to be bad. It's fascinating. You come into a room they've been in and see pieces of debris and try to figure out what you had that was made from wicker or what had been stuffed with fluff.

JULIE KLAM

I'm convinced that petting a puppy is good luck.

MEG DONOHUE

Buy a pup and your money will buy love unflinching.

RUDYARD KIPLING

The best way to get a puppy is to beg for a baby brother—and they'll settle for a puppy every time.

WINSTON PENDLETON

The biggest dog has been a pup.

JOAQUIN MILLER

I would recommend to those persons who are inclined to stagnate, whose blood is beginning to thicken sluggishly in their veins, to try keeping four dogs, two of which are puppies.

Elizabeth von Arnum

Whoever said you can't buy happiness forgot little puppies.

Gene Hill

The love of a dog is a pure thing. He gives you a trust which is total. You must not betray it.

Michel Houellebecq

"I'm not alone," said the boy. "I've got a puppy."

JANE THAYER

I am I because my little dog knows me.

GERTRUDE STEIN

There is no psychiatrist in the world like a puppy licking your face.

BEN WILLIAMS

Love is how excited your puppy gets when you get home.

AUTHOR UNKNOWN

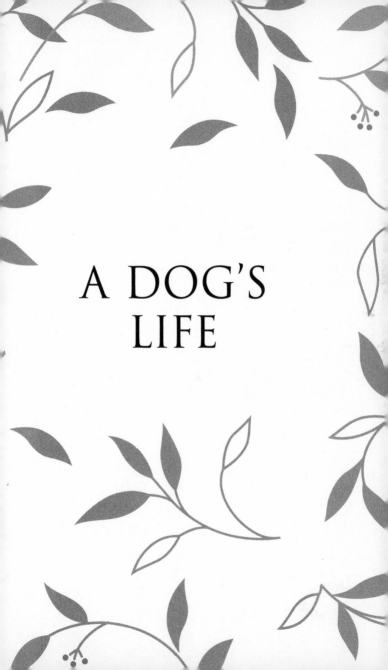

# A DOG'S LIFE

Like many other much-loved humans, they believed that they owned their dogs, instead of realizing that their dogs owned them.

D. Smith

Dogs are our link to paradise. They don't know evil or jealousy or discontent. To sit with a dog on a hillside on a glorious afternoon is to be back in Eden, where doing nothing was not boring—it was peace.

Milan Kundera

Dogs never bite me. Just humans.

MARILYN MONROE

Both humans and dogs love to play well into adulthood, and individuals from both species occasionally display evidence of having a conscience.

JON WINOKUR

A dog is not "almost human" and I know of no greater insult to the canine race than to describe it as such.

JOHN HOLMES

Why does watching a dog be a dog fill one with happiness?

JONATHAN SAFRAN FOER

All his life he tried to be a good person. Many times, however, he failed. For after all, he was only human. He wasn't a dog.

SNOOPY

A dog reflects the family life. Whoever saw a frisky dog in a gloomy family, or a sad dog in a happy one? Snarling people have snarling dogs, dangerous people have dangerous ones.

CONAN DOYLE

I don't judge others. I don't hate. I don't discriminate. I don't care about money. I don't hold grudges. I DO know how to love unconditionally and that's all I want in return. I'm a fur-ever friend.

AUTHOR UNKNOWN

While he has not, in my hearing, spoken the English language, he makes it perfectly plain that he understands it. And he uses his ears, tail, eyebrows, various rumbles and grunts, the slant of his great cold nose or a succession of heartrending sighs to get his meaning across.

JEAN LITTLE

I believe in integrity. Dogs have it. Humans are sometimes lacking it.

Cesar Millan

The dog has an absolutely uncanny knack of knowing what we are thinking, even of what we are feeling.

Brian Vesey-Fitzgerald

It is a truism to say that the dog is largely what his master makes of him: he can be savage and dangerous, untrustworthy, cringing and fearful; or he can be faithful and loyal, courageous and the best of companions and allies.

Sir Ranulph Fiennes

Once you have had a wonderful dog, a life without one, is a life diminished.

DEAN KOONTZ

In a perfect world, every dog would have a home and every home would have a dog.

AUTHOR UNKNOWN

Dogs' lives are too short. Their only fault, really.

AGNES SLIGH TURNBULL

Dogs don't lie. A dog's tail is a strikingly honest window to their souls.

JIM HILLIBISH

I like dogs. You always know what a dog is thinking. It has four moods. Happy, sad, cross and concentrating. Also, dogs are faithful and they do not tell lies because they cannot talk.

Mark Haddon

One could say that dogs see the world faster than we do, but what they really do is see just a bit more world in every second.

Alexandra Horowitz

When the world around me is going crazy and I'm losing faith in humanity, I just have to take one look at my dog to know that good still exists.

Author Unknown

A dog is like an eternal Peter Pan, a child who never grows old and who therefore is always available to love and be loved.

AARON KATCHER

Certainly they don't challenge you in the ways a spouse, parent or child can. But in their own way, they do get you to think beyond your own needs a little. If you don't believe that, try walking an unhappy dog at midnight in the pouring rain.

BOB MORRIS

The dog has an enviable mind; it remembers the nice things in life and quickly blots out the nasty.

BARBARA WOODHOUSE

The average dog is a nicer person than the average person.

Andy Rooney

Many of us have to spell words such as "out," "cookie," and "bath" when conversing with other people, lest we unnecessarily excite our pets. And even then they often understand. I've actually had clients who resorted to using a second language around their dogs, but after a while their perceptive pooches caught on. Who says dogs don't understand us?

Warren Eckstein

A dog wags its tail with its heart.

Martin Buxbaum

A dog can't think that much about what he's doing, he just does what feels right.

BARBARA KINGSOLVER

Ever wonder where you'd end up if you took your dog for a walk and never once pulled back on the leash?

ROBERT BRAULT

The intelligence of a Poodle and the loyalty of a Lassie. The bark of a Shepherd and the heart of a Saint Bernard. The spots of a Dalmatian, the size of a Schnauzer, and the speed of a Greyhound. A genuine, All-American Mutt has it all.

ASPCA SLOGAN

The average dog has one request to all humankind. Love me.

Helen Exley

To his dog, every man is Napoleon; hence the constant popularity of dogs.

Aldous Huxley

He wa'n't no common dog, he wa'n't no mongrel; he was a composite. A composite dog is a dog that is made up of all the valuable qualities that's in the dog breed—kind of a syndicate; and a mongrel is made up of all riffraff that's left over.

Mark Twain

After years of having a dog, you know him. You know the meaning of his snuffs and grunts and barks. Every twitch of the ears is a question or statement, every wag of the tail is an exclamation.

ROBERT McCAMMON

I am joy in a wooly coat, come to dance into your life, to make you laugh!

JULIE CHURCH

Money will buy you a pretty good dog, but it won't buy the wag of his tail.

JOSH BILLINGS

Old age means realizing you will never own all the dogs you wanted to.

Joe Gores

If you get to thinking you're a person of some influence, try ordering somebody else's dog around.

Will Rogers

A dog can express more with his tail in seconds than his owner can express with his tongue in hours.

Author Unknown

This soldier, I realized, must have had friends at home and in his regiment; yet he lay there deserted by all except his dog. I looked on, unmoved, at battles which decided the future of nations. Tearless, I had given orders which brought death to thousands. Yet here I was stirred, profoundly stirred, stirred to tears. And by what? By the grief of one dog.

Napoleon Bonaparte

No one appreciates the very special genius of your conversation as the dog does.

Christopher Morley

The better I get to know men, the more I find myself loving dogs.

Charles de Gaulle

If a dog will not come to you after having looked you in the face, you should go home and examine your conscience.

Woodrow Wilson

Any man with money to make the purchase can become dog's owner. But no man—spend he ever so much coin and food and tact in the effort—may become a dog's Master without the consent of the dog. Do you get the difference? And he whom a dog once unreservedly accepts as Master is forever that dog's God.

Albert Payson Terhune

# CANINE
# QUIPS

Every dog should have a man of his own. There is nothing like a well-behaved person around the house to spread the dog's blanket for him, or bring him his supper when he comes home man-tired at night.

Corey Ford

Dogs feel very strongly that they should always go with you in the car, in case the need should arise for them to bark violently at nothing right in your ear.

Dave Barry

The most affectionate creature in the world is a wet dog.

AMBROSE BIERCE

Dogs are animals that poop in public and you're supposed to pick it up. After a week of doing this, you've got to ask yourself, "Who's the real master in this relationship?"

ANTHONY GRIFFIN

In dog training, jerk is a noun, not a verb.

DR. DENNIS FETKO

If you are a dog and your owner suggests that you wear a sweater... suggest that he wear a tail.

FRAN LEBOWITZ

Every dog has his day, unless he loses his tail, then he has a weak-end.

JUNE CARTER CASH

Taking me for a walk and not letting me check stuff out. Exactly whose walk is it anyway?

ANONYMOUS DOG

I've seen a look in a dogs' eyes, a quickly vanishing look of amazed contempt, and I am convinced that basically dogs think humans are nuts.

JOHN STEINBECK

A dog is one of the remaining reasons why some people can be persuaded to go for a walk.

O.A. BATTISTA

Life is a series of dogs.

GEORGE CARLIN

When dogs leap onto your bed, it's because they adore being with you. When cats leap onto your bed, it's because they adore your bed.

Alisha Everett

The pug is living proof that God has a sense of humor.

Margo Kaufman

I am not your dog, but if every time you saw me, you gave me a backrub, I would run to greet you, too.

Robert Brault

A well-trained dog will make no attempt to share your lunch. He will just make you feel so guilty that you cannot enjoy it.

Helen Thomson

Dogs come when they're called. Cats take a message and get back to you later.

Mary Bly

The more I see of the representatives of the people, the more I admire my dogs.

Alphonse de Lamartine

If your dog is fat, you aren't getting enough exercise.

Author Unknown

Some of my best leading men have been dogs and horses.

ELIZABETH TAYLOR

Heaven goes by favor. If it went by merit, you would stay out and your dog would go in.

MARK TWAIN

Scratch a dog and you'll find a permanent job.

FRANKLIN P. JONES

Cleaning with dogs in your house is like brushing your teeth while eating Oreos.

AUTHOR UNKNOWN

The amount of time it takes for a dog to "do its business" is directly proportional to outside temperature + suitability of owner's outerwear.

BETSY CAÑAS GARMON

If you can look at a dog and not feel vicarious excitement and affection, you must be a cat.

CARRIE LATET

When a dog runs at you, whistle for him.

HENRY DAVID THOREAU

And he's housebroken—he's broken every room in the house!

JACK LALANNE

Behind every slightly confused looking dog there's a cat laughing maniacally.

AUTHOR UNKNOWN

I spilled spot remover on my dog. He's gone now.

STEVEN WRIGHT

Never stand between a dog and the hydrant.

JOHN PEERS

I used to look at [my dog] Smokey and think, "If you were a little smarter you could tell me what you were thinking," and he'd look at me like he was saying, "If you were a little smarter, I wouldn't have to."

FRED JUNGCLAUS

In order to keep a true perspective of one's importance, everyone should have a dog that will worship him and a cat that will ignore him.

DEREKE BRUCE

The objective is not so much to walk your dog, as it is to empty him.

DAVE BARRY

Let's examine the dog mind: Every time you come home, he thinks it's amazing. He can't believe that you've accomplished this again. You walk in the door. The joy of it almost kills him. "He's back again! It's that guy! It's that guy!"

JERRY SEINFELD

Did you ever notice when you blow in a dog's face he gets mad at you? But when you take him in a car he sticks his head out the window!

STEVE BLUESTONE

How many legs does a dog have if you call the tail a leg? Four. Calling a tail a leg doesn't make it a leg.

ABRAHAM LINCOLN

He is so shaggy. People are amazed when he gets up and they suddenly realize they have been talking to the wrong end.

ELIZABETH JONES

You can say any foolish thing to a dog, and the dog will give you a look that says, "Wow, you're right! I never would've thought of that!"

DAVE BARRY

Whoever said "let sleeping dogs lie" didn't sleep with dogs.

AUTHOR UNKNOWN

If you think dogs can't count, try putting three dog biscuits in your pocket and then give him only two of them.

PHIL PASTORET

People teach their dogs to sit; it's a trick. I've been sitting my whole life, and a dog has never looked at me as though he thought I was tricky.

MITCH HEDBERG

I have never met a dog I couldn't help; however, I have met humans who weren't willing to change.

CESAR MILLAN

I named my dog 'Stay' . . . so I can say
"Come here, Stay. Come here, Stay."

STEVEN WRIGHT

If you want the best seat in the house,
move the dog.

AUTHOR UNKNOWN

Anybody who doesn't know what soap
tastes like never washed a dog.

FRANKLIN P. JONES

# OUR BEST
# FRIEND

O Lord don't let me once forget,
How I love my trusty pet.
Help me learn to disregard,
Canine craters in my yard.
Show me how to be a buddy,
Even when my sofa's muddy.
Don't allow my pooch to munch,
Postal carriers for lunch.
Shield my neighbor's cat from view,
Guide my steps around the doo.
Train me not to curse and scowl,
When it's puppy's night to howl.
Grant I shan't awake in fear,
With a cold nose in my ear.

Give me patience without end,
Help me be 'A Dog's Best Friend!'

AUTHOR UNKNOWN,
Dog Owner's Prayer

Dogs have always been bred to be companions to humans. Our needs have changed now, and the roles they play are changing accordingly. We don't need them to help us find our food anymore. We need them to help us calm down.

STACY ALLDREDGE

If I had a dollar for every time my dog made me smile, I would be a millionaire.

AUTHOR UNKNOWN

...His head on my knee can heal my human hurts. His presence by my side is protection against my fears of dark and unknown things. He has promised to wait for me... whenever...wherever—in case I need him. And I expect I will—as I always have. He is just my dog.

GENE HILL

Before you get a dog, you can't quite imagine what living with one might be like; afterward, you can't imagine living any other way.

CAROLINE KNAPP

No matter how little money and how few possessions you own, having a dog makes you rich.

LOUIS SABIN

Dogs are not our whole life, but they make our lives whole.

ROGER CARAS

Petting, scratching, and cuddling a dog could be as soothing to the mind and heart as deep meditation and almost as good for the soul as prayer.

DEAN KOONTZ

I talk to him when I'm lonesome like; and I'm sure he understands. When he looks at me so attentively, and gently licks my hands; then he rubs his nose on my tailored clothes, but I never say naught thereat. For the good Lord knows I can buy more clothes, but never a friend like that.

W. Dayton Wedgefarth

When the Man wake up he said, 'What is Wild Dog doing here?' And the Woman said, 'His name is not Wild Dog any more, but the First Friend, because he will be our friend for always and always and always.'

Rudyard Kipling

The greatest pleasure of a dog is that you may make a fool of yourself with him and not only will he not scold you, but he will make a fool of himself too.

SAMUEL BUTLER

He is your friend, your partner,
    your defender, your dog.
You are his life, his love, his leader.
He will be yours, faithful and true,
To the last beat of his heart.
You owe it to him to be worthy of
    such devotion.

AUTHOR UNKNOWN

There is no faith which has never yet been broken, except that of a truly faithful dog.

KONRAD LORENZ

No one can fully understand the meaning of love unless he's owned a dog. A dog can show you more honest affection with a flick of his tail than a man can gather through a lifetime of handshakes.

GENE HILL

I like dogs better [than people]. They give you unconditional love. They either lick your face or bite you, but you always know where they're coming from. With people, you never know which ones will bite. The difference between dogs and men is that you know where dogs sleep at night.

GREG LOUGANIS

I think dogs are the most amazing creatures; they give unconditional love. For me
they are the role model for being alive.

Gilda Radner

Such short little lives our pets have to
spend with us, and they spend most of it
waiting for us to come home each day. It is
amazing how much love and laughter they
bring into our lives and even how much
closer we become with each other because
of them.

John Grogan

A dog is the only thing on earth that loves
you more than he loves himself.

Josh Billings

I have found that when you are deeply troubled, there are things you get from the silent devoted companionship of a dog that you can get from no other source.

DORIS DAY

The eyes of a dog, the expression of a dog, the warmly wagging tail of a dog and the gloriously cold damp nose of a dog were in my opinion all God-given for one purpose only—to make complete fools of us human beings.

BARBARA WOODHOUSE

My sunshine doesn't come from the skies,
It comes from the love in my dog's eyes.

UNKNOWN POET

The dog has been esteemed and loved by all the people on earth and he has deserved this affection for he renders services that have made him man's best friend.

ALFRED BARBOU

A person who has never owned a dog has missed a wonderful part of life.

BOB BARKER

Man himself cannot express love and humility by external signs, so plainly as does a dog, when with drooping ears, hanging lips, flexuous body, and wagging tail, he meets his beloved master.

CHARLES DARWIN

She had no particular breed in mind, no unusual requirements. Except the special sense of mutual recognition that tells dog and human they have both come to the right place.

LLOYD ALEXANDER

We long for an affection altogether ignorant of our faults. Heaven has accorded this to us in the uncritical canine attachment.

GEORGE ELIOT

His ears were often the first thing to catch my tears. [Referring to her cocker spaniel, Flush]

ELIZABETH BARRETT
BROWNING

When most of us talk to our dogs, we tend to forget they're not people.

JULIA GLASS

Dogs have a way of finding the people who need them, filling an emptiness we don't even know we have.

THOM JONES

The dog is the most faithful of animals and would be much esteemed were it not so common. Our Lord God has made his greatest gift the commonest.

MARTIN LUTHER

Thorns may hurt you, men desert you,
sunlight turn to fog; but you're never
friendless ever, if you have a dog.

DOUGLAS MALLOCK

Dogs, bless them, operate on the premise
that human beings are fragile and require
incessant applications of affection and
reassurance. The random lick of a hand
and the furry chin draped over the instep
are calculated to let the shaky owner know
that a friend is nearby.

MARY MCGRORY

Acquiring a dog may be the only opportunity a human ever has to choose a relative.

MORDECAI SIEGAL

The psychological and moral comfort of a presence at once humble and understanding—this is the greatest benefit that the dog has bestowed upon man.

PERCY BYSSHE SHELLEY

A dog doesn't care if you're rich or poor, big or small, young or old. He doesn't care if you're not smart, not popular, not a good joke-teller, not the best athlete, nor the best-looking person. To your dog, you are the greatest, the smartest, the nicest human being who was ever born. You are his friend and protector.

LOUIS SABIN

Usually they are quick to discover that I cannot see or hear....It is not training but love which impels them to break their silence about me with the thud of a tail rippling against my chair on gambols round the study, or news conveyed by expressive ear, nose, and paw. Often I yearn to give them speech, their motions are so eloquent with things they cannot say.

HELEN KELLER

"Hi," I said. She came over, licked my hand discreetly, allowed herself to be scratched for a time, chased her tail in a dignified circle, lay down again. I remember thinking: "There are times God puts a choice in front of you." I often had such thoughts back then. We took the dog.

STANLEY BING

When a puppy's eyes open it has a very strong ability to learn about people and... this behavior persists throughout life. And surprisingly, most dogs, given the choice, will actually prefer human company to other dog company.

JOHN BRADSHAW

The difference between friends and pets is that friends we allow into our company, pets we allow into our solitude.

ROBERT BRAULT

You're only a dog, old fellow;
a dog, and you've had your day;
But never a friend of all my friends
has been truer than you alway.

JULIAN STEARNS CUTLER

It's just the most amazing thing to love a dog, isn't it? It makes our relationships with people seem as boring as a bowl of oatmeal.

JOHN GROGAN

We give dogs time we can spare, space we can spare and love we can spare. And in return, dogs give us their all. It's the best deal man has ever made.

M. ACKLAM

We can judge the heart of a man by his treatment of animals.

IMMANUEL KANT

Love me, love my dog.

GEORGE CHAPMAN

# IRISh
## blessings, toasts
## & traditions

# IRISH
## BLESSINGS, toasts
## & traditions

EDITED BY
JASON S. ROBERTS

BARNES
&NOBLE
B O O K S
NEW YORK

# contents

# Introduction

Often it is said that the Irish are born with the gift of the blarney—and an Irishman can certainly tell a tale like no other. In the rich tradition of Irish lore and legend, tales of fairies with magical powers are the most common as well as the most enjoyable, for when fairies are present there is always the possibility of great fortune or unwitting disaster, not to mention a good story.

This delightful collection brings together the luck and charm of the Irish in a single volume filled with blessings, toasts, old-fashioned customs, sayings, superstitions, jokes, limericks, and legends.

Even throughout the Irish countryside today, simple gestures may be seen that are reminiscent of half-remembered rituals. Modern practices of all kinds can be traced back to old customs and traditions, and even old Irish sayings have a familiar ring.

You'll find common remedies for simple ailments such as headache, heartache, or freckles—and love spells using herbs and poetry, such as:

*Moon, moon tell unto me,*
*When my true love I shall see?*

*What fine clothes am I to wear?*
*How many children will I bear?*

*For if my love comes not to me,*
*Dark and dismal my life will be.*

Discover old Irish rituals such as jumping over a bonfire on Saint John's Day or protecting the butter from the Little People on May Day. Why did maidens hunt snails on May morning? Did bachelors have to stay out of sight on Ash Wednesday? Why was moving house on Saturday a bad idea? What would a maiden see in the mirror at midnight on Hallow Eve?

From the wailing and clapping of the Banshee to the dancing and whimsical pranks of the Little People, here are gems of Irish folklore and tradition guaranteed to enchant old and young alike.

# BLESSINGS

Chosen leaf
Of Bard and Chief,
Old Erin's native Shamrock!
Says Valour, "See
They spring for me
Those leafy gems of morning!"
Says Love, "No, No,
For me they grow,
My fragrant path adorning!"
But Wit perceives
The triple leaves,
And cries,—"O do not sever
A type that blends
Three godlike friends,
Love, Valour, Wit, for ever!
O! the Shamrock, the green, immortal
    Shamrock!"

May Christ and His saints stand
between you and harm.
Mary and her Son.
St. Patrick with his staff.
Martin with his mantle.
Bridget with her veil.
Michael with his shield.
And God over all with His strong right hand.

Three things are of God;
And these three are what Mary told to her Son,
For she heard them in heaven:

The merciful word;
The singing word;
And the good word.

May the power of these three holy things
Be on all the men and women of Erin for
evermore.

If a fairy, or a man, or a woman
  Hath overlooked thee,
  There are three greater in heaven
  Who will cast all evil from thee
  Into the great and terrible sea.
  Pray to them, and to the seven angels of God,
  And they will watch over thee.

Four corners to her bed
Four angels at her head
Mark, Matthew, Luke and John;
God bless the bed that she lies on.
New moon, new moon, God bless me
God bless this house and family.

# toasts

**h**ere's to absent friends and here's twice to absent enemies.

Here's to the light heart and the heavy hand.

Thirst is a shameless disease so here's to a shameful cure.

**h**ere's to a wet night and a dry morning.

May we always have a clean shirt, a clean conscience, and a bob in the pocket.

May you be across Heaven's threshold before the old boy knows you're dead.

# traditions

# may day

On May Day, the Skelligs sailed to meet the rocks opposite and the rocks did likewise, both retiring when they had touched. On May Day, sleeping out of doors was dangerous and the little people had a particularly detrimental effect on butter, on cream, on cows, and a host of other things. On the eve of May Day, cattle were driven into Cooey Bay from off Devenish Island to prevent their developing the dreaded cattle disease "murrain."

Bunches of flowers were gathered in the fields and, apart from those that found their way through young hands to adorn the gay "May Bush" in family gardens, they were crushed and used to bathe the udders of cows.

Pipes were never lit from the griosach (glowing red coals) of fire on May Day nor were embers ever taken outdoors.

Young damsels sometimes went hunting the snails in the grass on a dewy May morning. "The druchtin so caught shall be placed on a plate of flour," said the instructions, "and the snail will move around the flour leaving in its trail the name of the one to whom the fair maid will be wed."

Before sunrise on May morning, country people cut hazel rods out of which they carved small figures. They kept these in their stables or on their person to ward off evil.

The giving away of milk, always suspect, had further implications upon May Day, for whoever got milk of a cow first on that day received the profit from that cow for the remainder of the year. This belief was so strong that a court of law is said to have ruled in favor of a man who struck down an intruder in his byre on May Day, believing him to be after his milk.

A dying woman was refused milk on May Eve on one recorded occasion and a red-headed woman would not even be allowed to cross a threshold on May Day.

# christmas

On "Little Christmas," the feast of the Epiphany, the tail of a herring was rubbed across the eyes of a child to give immunity against disease for the remainder of the year.

On Christmas Day itself, it was most unusual for people to visit other households. This custom is still widely observed. The great feast really continued until St. Brigid's Day, when the straw from the nativity crib would be put away into the rafters as a protection against evil spirits or as a cure for ringworm. Holly, placed around the house as decoration for the season, was usually burnt under the pancakes being cooked on Shrove Tuesday, the eve of Ash Wednesday.

On Christmas Eve, the youngest child in the house was brought along to where the Christmas candle was placed waiting in the window and it was a most touching moment when the little one's tender hand was guided to light the symbol of welcome for the Holy Family.

Fish was a customary Christmas Eve meal. A special dish called priail, a white-sauce-coated fish, was popular.

Animals given the gift of speech, donkeys kneeling at midnight, exchanging gifts of farm produce, extra food given to animals, mummers, and "Wren Boys" on St. Stephen's Day, chimneys cleaned, all members of the family taking their turn at stirring the pudding—and turns by proxy for absent members: these were some of the customs associated with the season of Christmas before the tinsel and the paper chain, the Christmas tree, and the commercial excitement arrived. But happily, the homes of many country people still have the beckoning candle and a "Holy Night."

On the second day after Christmas, abstaining from meat served as a preventative against fever. This precaution seems singularly attractive, for doing without meat on the second day after Christmas would be a blessed relief.

Around the Rossnowlagh area of Donegal, on the twelfth night, a ritual almost like a seance was observed. A round cake, a flat container of dried mud, sand, or even animal dung was placed in the kitchen. A rush candle or a piece of bog-oak representing each member of the family was placed in the "cake" and lit. The lights were said to have become extinguished in the order that the members of the family would die.

# whitsuntide

Whitsuntide was associated with death by drowning. There were some who would not go to sea on that day unless the steady hand of a bride steered, and persons previously drowned were thought to make their return at Whitsuntide to enlist new victims for company.

Babies born then, it was said, would either kill or be killed unless a chicken was put into the infant's hand and it was made to squeeze the creature to death.

A foal born at Whitsuntide would either win a race or kill a man, and children often had their heads massaged with salt to prevent their being taken by the fairies.

# saint brigid's day

St. Brigid was loved by all Gael, and her cloak is said to have spanned the Curragh's vast plain.

Her feast day is on the first day of February and of spring. A doll representing the saint was carried about in some villages. This doll was called the "Brideog." A churn's dash was sometimes used to make the "Brideog," and all the women had to bow before it as it was paraded about the village. St. Brigid's day was the feast day when crosses woven from rushes on that eve were placed in tillage fields and in the rafters of cow-byres to bring good luck on the harvests.

Children laid beds of rushes pulled by hand in front of the fire on St. Brigid's eve in case the saint wished to rest during the night. Cutting the rushes with a knife was considered wrong.

The Brigid's cross tradition is said to have originated when a golden cross commemorating the saint was stolen and manifold weaving of the humble rush type replaced it.

# the season of lent

Shrove was the period preceding the penitential season of Lent and Shrove Tuesday, the day before Ash Wednesday. This was often called "Puss Wednesday" because girls who did not manage to get a husband during Shrove would have a "puss" on them on Ash Wednesday. It must be understood that marriages could not then take place during Lent, so if a ring wasn't tossed a girl's way along with a pancake she had a good seven weeks to go before she could marry.

In the port of Waterford there was a custom whereby bachelors and spinsters were often tied to a large log which was dragged along the quayside on Ash Wednesday. Graffiti, often gross or obscene, appeared on the doors of their houses, and the unfortunate people suffered great embarrassments because of their state.

Marriage was forbidden within the proscribed degrees of kindred or from Ash Wednesday to Trinity Sunday. Those who didn't make it during Shrove got suitably marked on "Chalk Sunday," the first Sunday in Lent. Mayo scribes did their marking on the first Monday in Lent and they took the added liberty of shaking salt on their victims.

Tying string to door knockers, climbing a roof and stuffing the chimney with a sack, taking gates off hinges and carrying them away—these were some of the other pranks played on bachelors and spinsters.

Good Friday, the day of our Savior's crucifixion was a day when little work was done in the countryside, although in some areas it was considered a lucky day to sow potatoes.

Using a hammer and nails was thought to be particularly unlucky.

On the east coast, boats in harbor would be left lying toward the quay wall on that day.

Persons who had "given up something" for Lent watched the clock tick away the last moments of Holy Saturday as they waited to indulge once again in their abandoned luxury.

Decorated eggs boiled in water in which the blossom of furze had been stewed were rolled down hillsides on Easter Monday. A cluideog (about a dozen) of eggs was a typical Easter present between country folk. Eggs and Easter were synonymous.

Blessing of stock, fields, or houses with the new Easter oils was greatly sought after.

# hallow eve

**t**he thirty-first of October is called Hallow Eve, Hallowe'en, All Souls, or Hollentide. But folk customs associated with this Eve of All Saints are more concerned with All Souls (November 2nd). It is a time of superstition, and of deep religious feelings for departed relatives and friends.

It was the period when the dead were said to exact revenge for ills done to them while on this earth, and when crosses were hung in their memory. A good fire was always left burning that night—for the fairies.

People avoided taking shortcuts across beaches, fields, or cliffs for fear the fairies would lead them astray.

Pairs of chestnuts left by the open fire to represent people about to be married were examined with deep anxiety—for if they stayed together on being heated then the couple would live together in harmony. But if they scattered apart there would be strife in that union.

A candle knocked over on Hallow Eve night was an ill-omen. Small piles of salt were often placed on a plate, each representing a member of the family.

A pile that caved in signified death within the year for its owner.

If a girl sat before a mirror eating an apple she would see the reflection of her future husband at midnight.

The custom of children dressing up and going around from door to door with the "Phooka" still survives, although it is not so much as to accompany the "Phooka" but with a firm intention of gleaning as much small change as possible from householders that children go out nowadays. The "Phooka" had various descriptions according to the part of the country, but he was usually described as a rather ugly-looking black horse.

The last night of November was said to be the closing night of the fairies' season of revelry. Better not be abroad on that night for the dead have their fling of dancing with the fairies on the hillsides while drinking their wine. Thereafter they get back into their coffins until the following November.

A foolish young lady, out late on such a night, sat down to rest and was approached by a young man who invited her to tarry awhile to see the magnificent dancing on the hillside. He looked pale and sad and she soon discovered that he was a young man who had been drowned while fishing the previous June. Furthermore the dancers that he showed her were all the dead she had known.

The young man warned her to get home quickly or she would be taken by the fairies to the dance and she would never return. His advice came too late, however. The dancers arrived, encircled her and whirled about until she dropped to the ground in a faint. That she managed to get home is certain for she was discovered the next morning in her own bed, pale and gaunt and it was pronounced that she had the "fairy stroke." The herb-doctor was called and every known antidote to the fairies' evil spell was employed but to no avail. The moon rose among dark clouds and slowly a quiet plaintive music was heard without. It grew louder, the moon became clouded and the young woman slowly passed on.

# saint John's day

St. John's Day falls on the twenty-fourth of June and its eve had certain customs associated with it. Sprigs of St. John's worth, an herb, were brought into homes. They were placed in windows to ward off evil, and berries from rowan trees tied to door-posts in stables or to masts of boats.

Bonfires were lit on that night and when the bonfires were dying down, cows were often driven through. Red embers from the fire had to be tossed about in tillage fields before retiring, however. The "Biltine" or lucky fire was really a pair of fires between which the cattle were driven to protect them against disease for the year.

In some areas young boys and girls would jump over the bonfires and the highest jumper would be the first to be married.

# odd days

**S**aturday's flitting, a short sitting," in other words, nobody moved house on a Saturday, got married on a Saturday, or embarked on any big project on the day before the Sabbath. Overnight travel was never undertaken.

Irish weather very often includes some very cold days at the beginning of April, just when mild, soft weather is expected. These days are said to be "borrowed from March" and they are called Laetheanta na Riaihe.

The "cold stone" was said to leave the water on St. Patrick's Day, March 17th. This merely meant that milder weather was coming. Present day resentment of Mondays stems mainly from over-indulgence in the good things of living, but Mondays have always been out of favor. It was unlucky to break anything, especially a cup, on Monday. If salt or tobacco were given on a Monday, the week's luck would be given with it.

The first Monday of the year was known as "Handsel Monday" and upon that day a dark-haired member of the family who had been unceremoniously instructed to leave the house just before midnight re-entered after the witching hour. This ensured that the dark-haired one, the harbinger of good luck, would be first into the home on Handsel Monday.

There were many occasions for refusing the incessant borrower in folklore. Although loaning was tolerated on Handsel Monday, giving away was not. If debts were paid on that day many more would be incurred throughout the year.

# superstitions

*Moon, moon tell unto me,*
*When my true love I shall see?*

*What fine clothes am I to wear?*
*How many children will I bear?*

*For if my love comes not to me,*
*Dark and dismal my life will be.*

This verse, recited by a maiden as she gathered special herbs by the light of the first full moon of the new year, could reveal a future husband and cause the girl to have a true dream about the man—if she first complied with certain requirements. With a black-handled knife she had to cut out three pieces of earth, bring them home, tie them in her left stocking, and secure the bundle with her right garter. The completed package then had to be placed under her pillow.

To cause love, keep a sprig of mint in your hand until the herb grows moist and warm, then take hold of the hand of the woman you love, and she will follow you as long as your two hands close over the herb. No invocation is necessary; but silence must be kept between the two parties for ten minutes, to give the charm time to work.

When yawning, make the sign of the cross instantly over your mouth, or the evil spirit will make a rush down and take up his abode with you.

Never disturb the swallows, wherever they may build, and neither remove nor destroy their nests; for they are wise birds, and will mark your conduct either for punishment or favor.

It is unlucky to offer your left hand in salutation, for there is an old saying: "A curse with the left hand to those we hate, but the right hand to those we honor."

**B**ad luck it is to take away a lighted sod on May Day or churning days; for fire is the most sacred of all things, and you remove the blessing from the house along with it.

If a man is ploughing, no one should cross the path of the horses.

If the palm of your hand itches you will be getting money; if the elbow, you will be changing beds.

**t**o throw a slipper after a party-going journey is lucky. Also to breakfast by candle-light on Christmas morning.

If a chair falls as a person rises, it is an unlucky omen.

It is very lucky for a hen and her chickens to stray into your house. Also it is good to meet a white lamb in the early morning with the sunlight on its face.

**B**y accident, if you find the back tooth of a horse, carry it about with you as long as you live, and you will never want money; but it must be found by chance.

If your ear itches and is red and hot, someone is speaking ill of you.

It is unlucky and a bad omen to carry fire out of a house where any one is ill.

*E*very day has one hour in which a wish may be granted and in which a person has the power to see spirits. Only by trial and error can that period be known.

A drink of distilled juice of the deadly night-shade will make a person believe anything if he is called upon from beneath a double-ended briar.

**a** red-haired woman is unlucky. Said to be typically Irish, red-haired women were nonetheless treated with great suspicion, and if a man met one as he was going to work he would almost certainly forget all about his labors and go home.

Whistling was considered unlucky under certain circumstances. Fishermen did not whistle on board nor did actors in their dressing-rooms.

**B**reaking a mirror brought seven years of bad luck, while two people washing hands in the same basin at the same time courted disaster.

The throwing of a pinch of salt over the shoulder was an antidote for all misfortunes.

The first person seen by a cat that has wiped its face with its paws may be the first of a household to die.

The liver of a black cat ground down to a powder and infused was said to be a powerful aphrodisiac and young maidens are said to have influenced wealthy playboys, while under the sway of cat liver, to make wild love and propose to them.

a purse made from the skin of a weasel would never be empty of money, yet weasels were often regarded as old and shrivelled witches, to be feared for their spiteful and vengeful ways. To meet a weasel was unlucky and to kill one disastrous—unless one's own hen was immediately killed in reparation, prayed over, and left hanging on a post in the haggard.

If the first lamb of the season was born black, it was thought to indicate that black mourning clothes would be worn by the family before the year ended.

For ordinary disease, there is nothing so good as the native poteen, for it is peculiarly adapted to the climate, and, as the people say, it keeps away ague and rheumatism, and the chill that strikes the heart; and if the gaugers would only let the private stills alone, not a bit of sickness would there be in the whole country round.

For ague, a few spiders tied up in a bag and worn round the neck will keep off the fever; but none, save the fairy doctor, must ever open the bag to look at the contents, or the charm will be broken.

For the memory, the whitest of frankincense beaten fine and drunk in white wine wonderfully assists the memory and is also profitable for the stomach.

For a nervous headache, measuring the head is much practiced. The measuring doctor has certain days for practicing his art, and receives or visits his patients on no other occasion. He first measures the head with a piece of tape above the ears and across the forehead, then from ear to ear over the crown of the head, then diagonally across the vertex. After this he uses strong compression with his hands, and declares that the head is "too open." And he mutters certain prayers and charms at the same time. This process is repeated for three days, until at last the doctor asserts that the head is closing and has grown much smaller—in proof he shows his measurements; and the cure is completed when he pronounces the head to be "quite closed," whereupon the headache immediately vanishes, and the patient is never troubled again.

To cure fever, place the patient on the sandy shore when the tide is coming in, and the retreating waves will carry away the disease and leave him well.

To cure tonsillitis, apply a stocking filled with hot potatoes to the throat.

or freckles, anoint the face with the blood of a bull or hare, and this will take away the freckles and make the skin fair and clear. The distilled water of walnuts is also good for this purpose.

For depression of heart, when a person becomes low and careless about everything, as if all vital strength and energy had gone, they are said to have got a fairy blast. And blast-water must be poured over the person by the hands of a fairy doctor while saying, "In the name of the saint with the sword, who has strength before God and stands at His right hand." Great care must be taken that no portion of the water is profaned, and whatever is left after the operation must be poured on the fire.

# tales

# ulick, aeneas,
and andy

**M**áire Bhuí Ní Laoire the poet was joined in butter with the Callaghans. Poets don't get up too early so that Máire was always running with the night, and it was dark one evening when she was going over to Callaghan's with her little keeler of butter on her head. When she was passing Gugane lake, whatever look she gave, the waters of the lake had parted and she saw the sun shining in the land below, the people working in the fields, the cars going down the road, and she could hear the birds singing and the bell ringing in the chapel. She knew that if she had a piece of steel to throw into the lake the waters would remain parted and she could walk down there and converse with the people below and find out what sort of story they had.

She remembered that there was a steel tip on the heel of her shoe, so she put the keeler of butter on the wall of the little bridge. But when she bent down to rip the lace she had to take her eyes off the lake, and when she looked up again the waters had closed in. She went up to Callaghan's and told them of the beautiful vision she had seen and how sad it was that the waters closing in had prevented her from going down to meet the people.

"Do you know," says Timmy Callaghan to her, "wouldn't the story be a lot worse if the waters closed in while you were below!"

At that time, because of the small holdings, you'd have three or more families joined in butter. The produce of one farm would not be sufficient to fill the firkin, which was a tub-like container sent to the butter market in Cork. Each family would bring their share of butter to your house this week, to my house next week and so on. I don't know how they kept track of the individual contributions to the firkin. It must have been a good system for it was said that the families joined in butter never fell out.

Pacing the firkin was a job for the women. They'd clear the kitchen table and on it they'd wash the butter and re-wash it in lovely spring water. Then with butter spades they'd blend the produce of the different farms, for there could be a variation in the color according to the amount of clover in the grass. And there's nothing worse than streaky butter! That done they'd add a touch of salt to keep the life in it, and a dash of saffron to heighten the color. When the firkin was packed and covered in muslin, the lid was put on and the hoops fastened down.

If there was any butter beyond the household needs left over the women would make it into little bricks shaped with the butter spade which had a flowery design cut into the face, and these prints of butter were put sitting in a fresh cabbage leaf and given to a poor person who had no cow of his own.

It would do your heart good to see the women working together. Young women walking barefoot on the wet floor, their clothes loose on them in the height of summer. Fine bouncing women with black curly heads and full of their pickey! God help the man that'd stray into that company, moreover, if he was of a shy disposition. And they'd laugh enough at him!

There were these three men, Ulick, Aeneas and Andy, fine big men with round faces like a full moon. They were always drowsy looking with heavy lids coming down over their eyes. They had enormous appetites and when they were full they'd fall asleep on the back of a harrow. They were like-able, easy going, sociable lads that would do any-thing for a laugh. One day in town they went into a shop in Henn Street and asked them for a yard of milk. The shopkeeper didn't turn a hair. You could be asked for anything in Killarney! He just dipped his finger in the churn and drew a line of milk a yard long on the counter.

"There ye are!" he said.

"Thanks very much," one of them says. "Roll it up and put it in a paper bag and we'll pay you for it!"

Brothers they were, Ulick, Aeneas and Andy. They had no mind for girls and some people said that it was from the father they brought that caper, for he didn't get married until he was over sixty. The father was an enormous size of a man. When he went to Wales in 1901 the Welsh government wouldn't let him down the mine in case he would block the shaft! "Did you come over in one piece," they wanted to know, "or were you assembled here?" He got drunk one night in Cardiff, and on his way home to his lodgings he fell into a cut stone horse-trough and fell asleep, his legs cocking out below and his head above. The water in the trough covered him from his neck to his knees but he didn't wake. That night the water froze making himself and the stone all the one piece. Even that didn't wake him! The tram cars in the morning, they used to make the devil's own clitter, woke him up. He got to his feet, noticed nothing, and made his way to a public house where he stood with his back to a roaring fire. Well a few minutes after he was the most surprised man in Europe when he heard the crash behind him. It took ten Welshmen to lift the horse trough out in the yard.

His three sons, Ulick, Aeneas and Andy went to the bog one day to cut a sleán of turf. Ulick was on the top sod, Aeneas benching and Andy spreading. The day turned very hot, and after the dinner they went into the cois, lay down on the fionnan and fell asleep. There they were lost to God and the world when three young lassies came racing down the bank full of devilment as all young girls used to be at the time. When they saw the three boyos below they jumped down into the cois and pulling three stems of ceann-bhan they began to tickle Ulick, Aeneas and Andy under their noses until they woke them up!

 And whatever came over Ulick, Aeneas and Andy, don't ask me, maybe it was the time of year, they fell head over heels in love with the young girls. What am I talking about! They followed them home every step of the way and told the girls' mother, that not one foot would they put outside the door until they got a promise of her three daughters in marriage. The old lady was huffy enough about it, saying that she had something better in mind for her daughters than to be marrying them off to farmers, and small farmers at that.

"And they are three refined ladies," says she, "that never wet their fingers only upstairs eating biscuits and looking out the top window!"

But the three daughters said they'd sooner Ulick, Aeneas and Andy than if three lords came jangling their spurs to the door for them. The old lady had to be satisfied with that, and the arrangements went ahead for the big day. That night the mother called in the three daughters and said to them:

"I have no fortune to give ye only one purse of gold but as that is too small to divide it between three, I'll give it all to whichever one of ye will make the biggest fool of her husband after ye are married."

We'll skip now until the day of the wedding. The three lads kept awake long enough to say "I do" in the chapel. At the wedding dance that evening, after a feed of roast goose washed down with an ocean of drink, when Ulick, Aeneas and Andy hit the hay they went into a deep coma! God help their wives! In the morning the lady who was married to Ulick when she couldn't wake her husband thought to herself, as there was nothing else doing, that she might as well have a shot at winning the purse of gold. She took scissors and cut off his hair and beard. Then she laddered him and shaved his head and face so close that the draught woke him! And when he opened his eyes after the feed of poitín the night before, he was as drunk as when he went to bed.

"Who are you?" his wife asked him.

"I'm Ulick," he said.

She took the looking glass off the wall and held it in front of his face. He came out of the bed and when he saw his bare frame, long and lanky and his shaved head in the glass, looking for all the world like an Aran Banner on top of a walking cane, he said:

"Well that's not me whoever it is!"

"And what are you doing here?" she wanted to know. "Clear off out of this house and don't come back until you find the man of the house!"

So off with him—isn't drink a fright—and he shouting, "Anyone here see Ulick! Anyone here see Ulick!"

Around dinner time the second daughter that was married to Aeneas tried to waken her husband. Not a gug out of him! She put her ear to his chest. Not a sound. If his heart was beating it was keeping fairly quiet about it. That he was warm was the only sign that he was alive! So with an eye on the purse of gold she went out next door where there was a card of a woman living, and the two of them got a habit; there used to be a habit in every house that time. With the scissors they cut the brown shroud up the back and fitted it nicely around the man in bed. They joined hands in prayer, entwined the rosary beads around his fingers, lit a couple of candles and put the word out that he was dead. Indeed herself went into mourning, wherever she got the black dress!

Later that same day the youngest girl that was married to Andy—having spent the whole night and part of the day in bed with him in the hope that he'd wake—got tired of it and went to see what the day was doing.

Like everyone else she heard the sad news and rushed back and began to shake her husband saying:

"Wake up! Wake up! Your brother is dead!"

"Which one of them?" says he, rising out of the bed.

"Aeneas," she told him. "He went class of a sudden too, so they're burying him in a hurry. Put on your clothes and straighten out or you'll be late for the funeral."

"My clothes," says he. "The Lord save us! Didn't

I throw my shirt and all my old duds into the fire thinking now that I was married I wouldn't have to get up anymore. What'll I put around me?"

"It is a poor head," his wife said, "that there isn't a plan in it! Come up here to the kitchen to me!"

He went up to her in his nakedness, and she melted down a basin of lard and rubbed it well into him all over! She went out then and she brought in the pluckings of a black and white goose and shook the feathers on the floor.

"Roll yourself in that now!" she said.

He did, and when he got up he wasn't like anything that anyone had ever before saw, and the only thing you could say about him was that he wasn't naked! Off out the door with him. He was late, for the funeral had left the house. He ran after it, and when the mourners looked around and saw the apparition behind, they dropped the coffin and ran. The coffin falling woke up the man inside! The lid flew off and when the "corpse" stood up and saw Andy in the feathers the legs gave under him with fright and he sank down into the coffin again.

Aeneas and Andy had hardly time to recognize each other when a man ran up shouting:

"Anyone here see Ulick? Did you see him, holy father?" thinking, when he saw Aeneas in the habit, that he was a friar!

"Aren't you Ulick?" they said. They were sobering up now. "Yerra, you're Ulick," Aeneas said, "we'd know you boiled in porridge!"

There they were looking at each other and wondering how they became so transmogrified. Was this what marriage had done to them? Then all of a sudden realizing the trick their wives had played on them, they got into a tearing temper, and decided there and then that they'd go up to their mother-in-law's and wreck the house on her for landing them with three such mopsies of daughters. But when they went in above their wives were sitting inside before them, so they said nothing!

"There they are now, mother," says the daughters. "You see the cut of them, that's the result of the caper. It would be time for you to be delivering your judgement!"

The old lady stood up and she wasn't long about it. Looking at Ulick she said, "Samson lost his hair!" Looking at Aeneas she said, "Lazarus is risen from the dead!" And looking at Andy she burst out laughing, "The purse of gold," she said, "goes to my youngest daughter. It is a simple thing to make a fool of a man but it takes a bit of ingenuity to make a goose of him!"

# it snowed that night

there were these two poets and they used to go every year to the winter fair in Kenmare to buy two cows for the tub. When the deal was done they'd tie the two cows to the lamp post and go into the pub, where they'd spend the day and portion of the night arguing, insulting people they didn't like and exchanging verses. When they'd come out bye an' bye they wouldn't be cold but the two cows would be perished. When they'd rip the ropes off their horns the cows'd gallop off to get the blood back into circulation.

Now, it so happened one year that the poets bought two black cows, and when they got out of the light of the town, the night was so dark and the cows so black, that the poets couldn't see a splink. There they were with two ashplants running up and down, hether and over, in gaps and out gates after the cows. They could only go by the sound, so when they heard anything they'd draw with the ash plants and were hitting one another as often as not.

They spent the night on the road, up bohereens and into fields, and when it brightened in the morning they were driving two animals before them! Not their own I'm afraid. Two rangey bullocks belonging to some farmer in the Roughty Valley. By the time they had the bullocks restored to their rightful owners, by the time they had gone around to all the schools and made public the fact that the cows had strayed, and by the time they had found them, they swore they would never again get into such a mix-up of an adventure if they could at all avoid it.

Time moved on and the winter fair in Kenmare came around again, and neighbors were surprised to see the two poets late at night in a public house and they maith go leor!

"It is none of our business," the neighbors remarked among themselves, remembering the fools the poets made of themselves in the dark the year before. "Yerra let 'em at it!"

Drink or no drink you couldn't be ikey enough for poets. They got an inkling they were being talked about so one of 'em got up and sang,

> *We don't give a tráithnín about darkness,*
> *Be it blacker than nature allows.*
> *We're prepared for it this time, my buckos,*
> *We've purchased two handsome white cows.*

It snowed that night!

# fairies or no fairies

John Mulligan believed devoutly in fairies, and an angry man was he if you doubted them. He had more fairy stories than would make two thick quartos, all of which he used to tell on any occasion that he could find listeners. Many believed his stories—many more did not believe them—but nobody, in process of time, used to contradict the old gentleman, for it was a pity to vex him. But he had a couple of young neighbors who were just come down from their first vacation in Trinity College to spend the summer with their uncle Mr. Whaley, and they were too full of logic to let the old man have his own way undisputed.

Every story he told they laughed at, and said that it was impossible—that it was merely old woman's gabble, and such other things. When he would insist that all his stories were derived from the most credible sources—nay, that some of them had been told by his own grandmother, a very respectable old lady, but slightly affected in her faculties, as things that came under her own knowledge—they cut the matter short by declaring that she was in her dotage, and at best of times had a strong propensity to pulling a long bow.

"But," said they, "Jack Mulligan, did you ever see a fairy yourself?"

"Never," was the reply.

"Well, then," they answered, "until you do, do not be bothering us with any more tales of my grandmother."

That evening—it was at their uncle's, an old crony of his with whom he had dined—Jack Mulligan had taken a large portion of his usual beverage, and was quite riotous. He at last got up in a passion, ordered his horse, and, in spite of his host's entreaties, galloped off, although he had intended to have slept there, declaring that he would not have any thing more to do with a pair of jackanapes puppies, who, because they had learned how to read good-for-nothing books in cramp writing, and were taught by a parcel of wiggy, red-snouted, prating prigs, they imagined they knew more than a man who has held buckle and tongue together facing the wind of the world for five dozen years.

He rode off in a fret, and galloped as hard as his horse Shaunbuie could powder away over the limestone. "Damn it!" hiccuped he, "Lord pardon me for swearing! the brats had me in one thing—I never did see a fairy, and I would give up five as good acres as ever grew apple-potatoes to get a glimpse of one—and, by the powers! What is that?"

He looked and saw a gallant spectacle. His road lay by a noble demesne, gracefully sprinkled with trees, not thickly planted as in a dark forest, but disposed, now in clumps of five or six, now standing singly, towering over the plain of verdure around them, as a beautiful promontory arising out of the sea. He had come right opposite the glory of the wood. It was an oak called the old oak of Ballinhassig. Age had hollowed its center, but its mossy boughs still waved with their dark serrated foliage. The moon was shining on it bright. By this light Jack saw a brilliant company of lovely little forms dancing under the oak with an unsteady and rolling motion. Some spread out far beyond the farthest boundary of the shadow of the oak's branches—some were seen glancing through the flashes of light shining through its leaves—some were barely visible, nestling under the trunk—some no doubt were entirely concealed from his eyes. Never did man see any thing more beautiful. They were not three inches in height, but they were white as the driven snow, and beyond number numberless. Jack surveyed, with infinite delight, their diversified gambols. By looking long at them, he soon saw objects which had not struck him at first, in particular that in the middle was a chief of superior stature, round whom the group appeared to move. He gazed so long that he was quite overcome with joy, and could not help shouting out. "Bravo! little fellow," said he, "well kicked and strong." But the instant he uttered the words the night was darkened, and the fairies vanished with the speed of lightning.

"I wish," said Jack, "I held my tongue, but no matter now. I shall just turn to bridle about and go back to Ballybegmullinahone Castle, and beat the young Master Whaleys, fine reasoners as they think themselves, out of the field clean."

No sooner said than done, Jack was back again as if upon the wings of the wind. He rapped fiercely at the door, and called aloud.

"Halloo!" said he, "young Flatcaps, come down now, if you are. Come down, if you dare, and I shall give you ocular demonstration of the truth of what I was saying."

Off they rode, and soon came to the demesne of Oakwood. They arrived at the wall flanking the field where stood the great oak, and the moon, by this time, having again emerged from the clouds, shone bright as when Jack had passed. "Look there," he cried, exultingly, for the same spectacle again caught his eyes, and he pointed to it with his horsewhip, "look, and deny if you can."

"Why," said one of the lads, pausing, "true it is that we do see a company of white creatures, but were they fairies ten times over. I shall go among them," and he dismounted to climb over the wall.

"Ah, Tom! Tom!" cried Jack, "stop, man, stop! what are you doing? The fairies—the good people, I mean—hate to be meddled with. You will be pinched or blinded, or your horse will cast its shoe, or look! a wilful man will have his way. Oh! oh! he is almost at the oak—God help him! for he is past the help of man."

By this time Tom was under the tree, and burst out laughing. "Jack," said he, "keep your prayers to yourself. Your fairies are not bad at all. Believe they will make tolerably good catsup."

"Catsup," said Jack, who, when he found that the two lads (for the second had followed his brother) were both laughing in the middle of the fairies, had dismounted and advanced slowly—"What do you mean by catsup?"

"Nothing," replied Tom, "but that they are mushrooms (as indeed they were), and your Oberon is merely this overgrown puff-ball."

Poor Mulligan gave a long whistle of amazement, staggered back to his horse without saying a word, and rode home in a hard gallop, never looking behind him. Many a long day was it before he ventured to face the laughers at Ballybegmullinahone, and to the day of his death the people of the parish, ay, and five parishes round, called him nothing but Musharoon Jack, such being their pronunciation of mushroom.

# ∂aniel o'connell
## an∂ the colonel from battersea

**t**he Cork butter market, in its hey day, was the biggest in the world and it was said to grease the axel of the entire British army. You'd go up Shandon Street to it. It was like a bee-hive, well a cruiceog for it was round, with all the activity of buying and sampling and weighing and grading and testing. There was a man then with a fakah like an auger which he'd drive into the firkin and when he pulled it up, he had a cross section of what was inside. He'd run it across his nose tasting it with his tongue— what a job to have!—to see if it was all of equal quality and that there was nothing rancid at the bottom, and you were paid according to his pronouncement. The butter market made Cork, gave plenty of work and made the merchants rich. And one of those merchants went up for election one time; the opposition said he wouldn't get in, but his followers said he would.

"For," says they, "we'll graze his arse with butter and we'll skeet him to the top of the poll!"

It wasn't a landslide but he slipped in!

Butter was going to Cork from every corner of

Munster on horse back long before the roads were made. Squads of men would set out from as far south as Cahirciveen, and one horse would be loaded down with food for the journey. Later on when the coach roads were developed the car men came. They were a hardy breed of lads, and my own great grandfather was one. And they'd take as much as a horse and cart could carry of butter to the city and they'd bring back goods to be sold in the local shops when they were coming.

All that long journey could not be done in a day, so the butter men had special houses, in places like Carriganime, where horses and men could rest the night. These were houses where stories of the past and the present were exchanged, and every man would bring home a head full of news about the heroes of the day.

Daniel O'Connell was over in London at the time and he was staying in this hotel called the Royal Victoria. He was having his dinner one day surrounded by a lot of rich people. They didn't think very highly of Dan, for it was well known that Daniel O'Connell was on the side of the poor. Wasn't it the poor people that put him into parliament the first day. And another thing, at the time Dan used to defend people in court that broke the

English law, and because of that, I can tell you, he had very few friends in the city of London. During the course of the meal Dan, maybe he had a sup in, had occasion to go out the back. And while he was outside what did this fellow that was sitting alongside him do but spill the contents of a packet of white powder into Daniel O'Connell's cup! The servant girl was there and spotted it, and when Daniel O'Connell came back she said:

> "A Dhónail Uí Chonaill,
> A dtuigeann tú Gaoluinn?"
> "Tuigim go maith," duirt sé,
> "A chailín o Éirinn."
> Agus ar sise:
> "Tá nimh id chupán a leagadh na céadta!"
> "Más fíor san, a chailín," duirt sé,
> "is mór é do spré-sa!"

["O, Daniel O'Connell/do you understand Irish?"/"I do, and well," he said/"O, girl from Ireland."/And she said, "There's (enough) poison in your cup to stretch hundreds."/"If that's true," said he, "your dowry will be great."]

And she told him then in Irish, Irish is handy abroad! She told him that she saw this fellow, seanachornal ó Bhattersea a bhí ann, putting white powder into his cup. With that there was a great commotion outside in the street, shouting and cheering. Queen Victoria that was passing down, so all the quality ran over to look out the window. When there was no one watching him what did Daniel O'Connell do but exchange the cups, so when this old lad from Battersea came back he took the cup with the poison in it and drank it down. He died on the spot! Thanks be to God that Dan came safe out of it. Daniel O'Connell wiped his mouth and wrote out a check for the servant girl. He went out then taking the air for himself. He was going along when this giobhlachan came after him jeering him and singing a disparaging rocan,

*A Dhónail Uí Chonaill M.P. mar eadh!*
*Taoi i bhfad ó do mhuintir san áit seo.*
*Teir ar ais go hUíbh Ráthach,*
*Dos na prátaí is bláthach,*
*Is fág an áit seo do na huaisle!*

[O Daniel O'Connell M.P./you're a long way from your people in this place/go back to Ivearagh/to

63

the spuds and the buttermilk/ and leave this place to the nobles.]

Daniel eyed the singer and enquired, "An Ciarraioch tusa?"

"O sea," he said.

Duine de mhuintir Coffey?" says Dan. The Coffey's were of the traveling class.

"O sea," he said. "Is mise Dydeo."

["Are you a Kerryman?"/"I am," he said./"One of the Coffey's?" says Dan./"Yes," says he, "I'm Dydeo!"]

"I know your clann very well," says Dan. "I know ye all. Often I saw ye on the road from Castleisland down to Cahirciveen. Tell me this Dydeo. Who put you up to sing that piece of ráiméis for me?"

"Twas the owner of that hotel over there, the Royal Victoria. "Sing anything you have handy in Irish for Daniel O'Connell," says he, "and you'll get money from him!"'

"Oh, you'll get money all right," says Dan, "but it won't come from me! Come over here!"

And he brought Dydeo into a barber's shop where he got the man to give him a good clip and shave and to powder him up. Then he took Dydeo into a haberdashery. "Formal Wear" was written over the door, where Daniel O'Connell fitted Dydeo from the skin out in what was the height of fashion at the time. A tall silk hat, a cravat, a cut-away coat, patent leather shoes and when he came out carrying a walking cane and wearing a "glass eye" Dydeo looked a real gentleman!

Then Daniel O'Connell says to him:

"There's a fist-full of money for you now, and go back, down to the hotel, find the owner and rent a room from him for the space of a week. Be sure to bring me back a document signed by the owner to show that all is legal. And come here," says Dan to Dydeo tutoring him up and showing him how to walk with a nice measured pace. "Be very careful of your speech. Don't open your mouth over big when you're talking and keep the tone a little bit down out of your head! Say that you are from Siam and that your wives are coming this evening!"

Aren't they broadminded in London! Imagine bringing a squad of wives into a hotel in Tralee.

Off with Dydeo, and do you know, when you're in the right clothes it is easy enough to fool people. Dydeo came back in no time with the document signed and ready for occupation. Dan ran his eye over the paper.

"That's fine," he said. "Keep it safe. Where's the

rest of the clann? I don't see them around."

"There's only the one place they'd be now," says Dydeo, "and that's above in Dirty Dick's in Cricklewood."

"Off with you up so," says Dan, "and get all your friends, men, women, and children to come down to the hotel and take over that room you are entitled to."

Away with Dydeo up to Cricklewood and when he went onto the public house above of course he thought no one would know him in fine clothes. Mo léir when he walked in the door they all stood up and burst out laughing.

"Come out from under the hat," they said, "we know your legs."

He told them of the plan and they collected up the pots and the pans, the canteens and the tin, the clippers and the timber hammers, and men, women and children came down in a body, down to the hotel. They went in the door and up the stairs and into the room, and they weren't a second inside when they began clouting tin, and the like of it for a clismirt was never heard before or since in the city of London.

The quality were having their dinner downstairs and the noise knocked such a start out of them that the food went down the wrong passage. The owner ran up the steps when he heard the clitter, and when he beheld the state of the room and saw what was happening inside, he rushed over to the window and called a squad of police that was passing outside. Now, it was a man called Sullivan, one of the black Sullivans from between Listry and Lisaphooka, that was over the police in London at the time. The minute he walked into the room and saw the Coffeys he knew who had, and going over to Dydeo he said to him in a very threatening tone, "You'll g'out of it!"

"I wo'not," said Dydeo, "g'out of it!"

And Sullivan shoving his jaw into Dydeo's face said to him again, "You'll g'out of it now!"

"I wo'not," Dydeo told him, "g'out of it now or any other time. I've this room rented for a week, as I have a contract to make saucepans for the British army. Take a look at that paper," giving the agreement signed by the owner to Sullivan. The policeman ran his eye down the paper and as he read it his face fell. Then turning to the owner he said, "This document is pure legal. They can't be evacuated for a week!"

The owner went into a reel and began kicking the wall with the dint of bad temper.

"I'll be ruined," he said, "by that time. The quality are moving out already!"

"Well," says Sullivan, a man well up in the matter of bribery, "if you want the custom of your lords and ladies gay you know what to do," and he winked at him and gave him the nod, so the owner drew Dydeo aside and asked him, would he evacuate for a consideration and Dydeo answered that that depended on the size of the consideration! The bargaining began and they went from a pound to two pounds to four pounds and Dydeo and the clann didn't put a foot outside the door until everyone got a fistful of notes. Then they gathered up the pots and the pans, the canteens and the tin, the clippers and the timber hammers and went down the stairs and out into the street. There was Daniel O'Connell outside on the flags waiting for them and a big clab on him laughing!

Dydeo looked at the money and then at the heavens saying, "God direct us where will we go, Cricklewood or Castleisland?"

"There's a better kick," says Dan, "off the stuff in Castleisland."

So they hit Fishguard and took the tub to Cork singing as they went:

*O Oileán Chiarraí mo mhuintear-sa*
*Ach i nGort an tSleibhe a rugadh mé*
*I bpoll fé'n chlaí go moch san oích'*
*'S narbh dheas an féirin dom mhamaí mé!*

[My people came from Castleisland/But I was born
in Gort a'tSléibhe/in a hole under a hedge early in
the night/And wasn't I the fine gift for my mother!]

# hudden, dudden and donald o'nery

hudden and Dudden and Donald O'Nery were near neighbors in the barony of Balinconlig, and ploughed with three bullocks; but the two former, envying the present prosperity of the latter, determined to kill his bullock, to prevent his farm being properly cultivated and labored, that going back in the world he might be induced to sell his lands, which they meant to get possession of.

Poor Donald O'Nery finding his bullock killed, immediately skinned it, and throwing the skin over his shoulder, with the fleshy side out, set off to the next town with it, to dispose of it to the best of his advantage. Going along the road a magpie flew on the top of the hide, and began picking it, chattering all the time. The bird had been taught to speak, and imitate the human voice, and Donald thinking he understood some words it was saying, put round his hand and caught hold of it. Having got possession of it, he put it under his coat, and so went on to the town.

Having sold the hide he went into an inn to take a dram, and following the landlady into the cellar, he gave the bird a squeeze which made it chatter some broken accents that surprised her very much.

"What is that I hear?" said she to Donald. "I think it is talk and yet I do not understand."

"Indeed," said Donald, "it is a bird I have and it tells me everything and I always carry it with me to know when there is danger. Faith," says he, "it says you have far better liquor than you are giving me."

"That is strange," said she, going to another cask of better quality, and asking him if he would sell the bird.

"I will," said Donald, "if I get enough for it."

"I will fill your hat with silver if you leave it with me."

Donald was glad to hear the news, and taking the silver set off, rejoiced at his good luck. He had not been long at home until he met with Hudden and Dudden. "Mr.," said he, "you thought you did me a bad turn, but you could not have done me better; for look here what I have got for the hide"—showing him the hatful of silver—"you never saw such a demand for hides in your life as there is at present."

Hudden and Dudden that very night killed their bullocks, and set out the next morning to sell their hides. On coming to the place they went through all the merchants, but could only get a trifle for them. At last, they had to take what they could get, and came home in a great rage, and vowing revenge on poor Donald.

He had a pretty good guess how matters would turn out, and being under the kitchen window, he was afraid they would rob him, or perhaps kill him when asleep, and on that account when he was going to bed he left his old mother in his place, and lay down in her bed, which was in the other side of the house, and taking the old woman for Donald, they choked her in her bed, but he making some noise they had to retreat, and leave the money behind them, which grieved them very much.

However, by day-break, Donald got his mother on his back, and carried her to town. Stopping at a well, he fixed his mother with her staff, as if she was stooping for a drink, and then went into a public-house convenient and called for a dram.

"I wish," said he to a woman that stood near him, "you would tell my mother to come in. She is at yon well trying to get a drink, and she is hard of hearing; if she does not observe you, give her a little shake and tell her that I want her."

The woman called her several times, but she seemed to take no notice; at length she went to her and shook her by the arm, but when she let her go again, she tumbled on her head into the well, and as the woman thought was drowned. She in great surprise and fear at the accident, told Donald what had happened.

"O mercy," said he, "what is this?"

"He ran and pulled her out of the well, weeping and lamenting all the time, and acting in such a manner that you would imagine he had lost his senses. The woman on the other hand was far worse than Donald, for his grief was only feigned, but she imagined herself to be the cause of the old woman's death.

The inhabitants of the town hearing what had happened, agreed to make Donald up a good sum of money for his loss, as the accident happened in their place, and Donald brought a greater sum home with him than he got for the magpie. They buried Donald's mother, and as soon as he was with Hudden and Dudden he showed them the last purse of money he had got.

"You thought to kill me last night," said he, "but it was good for me it happened on my mother, for I got all that purse for her to make gunpowder."

That very night Hudden and Dudden killed their mothers, and the next morning set off with them to town. On coming to the town with their burthen on their backs, they went up and down crying, "Who will buy old wives for gunpowder?" so that everyone laughed at them, and the boys at last clodded them out of the place.

Then they saw the cheat, and vowing revenge on Donald, buried the old women, and set off in pursuit of him. Coming to his house, they found him sitting at his breakfast, and seizing him, put him in a sack, and went to drown him in a river at some distance.

As they were going along the highway, they raised a hare, which they saw had but three feet, and throwing off the sack ran after her, thinking by appearance she would be easily taken. In their absence there came a drover that way and hearing Donald singing in the sack, wondered greatly what could be the matter.

"What is the reason," said he, "that you are singing, and you confined?"

"Oh, I am going to heaven," said Donald, "and in a short time I expect to be free from troubles."

"Oh dear," said the drover, "what will I give you, if you let me to take your place?"

"Indeed I do not know," said he, "it would take a good sum."

"I have not much money," said the drover, "but I have twenty head of fine cattle, which I will give you to exchange places with me."

"Well," says Donald, "I do not care if I should, loose the sack and I will come out."

In a moment the drover liberated him, and went into the sack himself, and Donald drove home the fine heifers, and left them in his pasture. Hudden and Dudden having caught the hare returned, and getting the sack on one of their backs carried Donald, as they thought, to the river and threw him in, where he immediately sunk. They then marched home intending to take immediate possession of Donald's property, but how great was their surprise when they found him safe at home before them, with such a fine herd of cattle, whereas they knew he had none before.

"Donald," they said, "what is all this? We thought you were drowned and yet you are here before us."

"Ah," he said, "if I had but help along with me when you threw me in, it would have been the best job ever I met with, for of all the sight of cattle, and gold that ever was seen is there, and no one to own them, but I was not able to manage more than what you see, and I could show you the spot where you might get hundreds."

They both swore they would be his friends, and Donald accordingly led them to a very deep part of the river, and lifted up a stone.

"Now," said he, "watch this"—throwing it into the stream— "there is the very place, and go in one of you first, and if you want help you have nothing to do but call."

Hudden jumping in, and sinking to the bottom, rose up again, and making a bubbling noise, as those do that are drowning, attempting to speak, but could not.

"What is that he is saying now?" says Dudden.

"Faith," says Donald, "he is calling for help, don't you hear him? Stand about," said he running back, "till I leap in. I know better how to do than any of you."

Dudden to have the advantage of him, jumped in off the bank, and was drowned along with Hudden, and this was the end of Hudden and Dudden.

# the man who had
# no story

**W**ell, there was a man down here in Barr an Ghaoith a long time ago and his name was Brian Ó Braonacháin. The trade that he had was cutting rods, making baskets of them and selling them in Glenties and in Dunloe and in Fintown and everywhere he could get them sold.

But one year he was down here and there wasn't a single rod in the whole of Barr an Ghaoith that he hadn't cut, made baskets of, sold and then spent the money. Those were bad times—the English were in power and they wouldn't let the Irish earn a single penny in any way. And Brian didn't know what to do.

In those days there was a little glen outside of Barr an Ghaoith that they called Alt an Torr and there were remarkable fine rods growing there. Nobody dared cut any of these rods, for everyone made out that it was a fairy glen. One morning Brian said to his wife that if she made him up a little lunch he would go out and cut the makings of a couple of baskets and perhaps no harm would come to him. The wife got up and made up a lunch

77

for him. He put it in his pocket and he took a hook and a rope under his arm.

He went out to the glen and he wasn't long in the glen until he had cut two fine bundles of rods. When he was tying them together so that he could carry them with the rope on his back, a terrible fog started to gather around him. He decided that he would sit down and eat his lunch and perhaps the fog would clear. He sat down and when he had finished eating it was so dark that he could not see his finger in front of him.

He stood up and he got terribly scared. He looked to the east and he looked to the west and he saw a light. When there is light, there must be people, he thought, and he headed for the light. He tripped and fell the whole time, but in the end he came up to the light. There was a big long house there. The door was open and there was a fine light coming out of the window and the door. He put his head in the door and an old woman was sitting in the corner and an old man on the other side of the fire. Both of them saluted Brian Ó Braonacháin from Barr an Ghaoith and wished him welcome, and they asked him to come up and sit in at the fire. Brian came up and he sat in at the fire between the pair of them. But he had not been sitting there long when the old man asked him to tell a fairy tale.

"That is something I never did in my whole life," said Brian, "tell a story of any kind. I can't tell Fenian tales or fairy tales of any kind."

"Well," said the old woman, "take that bucket and go down to the well below the house and fetch a bucket of water and do something for your keep."

"I'll do anything," said Brian, "except tell a story."

He took the bucket, went down to the well and filled it with water from the well. He left it standing on the flagstone beside the well, so that the water would run off it, before he brought it in. But a big blast of wind came and he was swept off up into the sky. He was blown east and he was blown west and when he fell to the ground he could see neither the bucket nor the well nor anything at all. He looked around and he saw a light and he made out that where there was light there must be people and headed for the light. He tripped and fell the whole time, it was so dark. But at last he came to the light. There was a big long house there, far bigger than the first house, two lights in it and a fine light out of the door.

He had put his head on the door, and what was it but a wake-house. There was a row of men sitting by the back wall of the house and a row of men sitting by the front wall of the house and up at the fire there was a girl with curly black hair sitting on a chair. She saluted and welcomed Brian Ó Braonacháin from Barr an Ghaoith and she asked him to come up and sit beside her on the chair. Brian came up and he sat down beside her and very shy he was, too. But he had not been sitting long when a big man who was in the company stood up.

"It is a very lonely wake we are having here tonight," said he, "a couple of us must go to get a fiddler, so that we can start dancing."

"Oh," said the girl with the curly black hair, "you don't have to go for any fiddler tonight," said she, "you have the best fiddler in Ireland among you here tonight, Brian Ó Braonacháin from Barr an Ghaoith."

"Oh, that is something I never did in my life," said Brian, "play a tune on a fiddle, and there is no music or singing or fiddling of any kind in my head."

"Oh," said she, "don't make me a liar, you are the very man who can fiddle."

Before Brian knew he had the bow and the fiddle in his hand and he played away and they danced away, and they all said that they had never heard any fiddler playing a tune on a fiddle better than Brian Ó Braonacháin from Barr an Ghaoith.

A big man who was in the company stood up and said that the dancing must stop now. "A couple of us must go for the priest, so that we can say Mass," said he, "for this corpse must go out of here before daybreak."

"Oh," said the girl with the curly dark hair, "there is no need to go for any priest tonight, the best priest in Ireland is sitting here beside me on the chair, Brian Ó Braonacháin from Barr an Ghaoith."

"Oh, I have nothing of a priest's power or holiness," said Brian, "and I do not know anything about a priest's work in any way."

"Come, come," said she. "You will do that just as well as you did the rest."

"Before Brian knew he was standing at the altar with two clerks and with the vestments on him. He started to say Mass and he gave out the prayers after Mass. And the whole congregation that was listening said that they never heard any priest in Ireland giving out prayers better than Brian Ó Braonacháin. Then the corpse was placed in a coffin outside the door and four men hoisted it on their shoulders. There were three fairly short men and one big tall man and the coffin was terribly shaky.

"One or two of us," said the big man who was in the company, "must go for a doctor so that we can cut a piece off the legs of that big man to make him level with the other three."

"Oh," said the girl with the curly black hair, "you don't need to go for any doctor tonight, the best doctor in Ireland is here among you tonight, Brian Ó Braonacháin from Barr an Ghaoith."

"Oh, that is something I never did in my life," said Brian, "doctoring of any sort, I never got any doctor's schooling at all."

"You'll do that just as well as you did the rest," said she.

"The lances were given to Brian and he cut a piece off the big man's legs, under his knees, and he stuck the legs back on, and he made him level with the other three men. Then they put the coffin on their shoulders and they walked gently and carefully west, until they came to the graveyard. There was a big stone-wall around it, ten feet high, or maybe twelve and they had to lift one man up on the wall first and they were going up one by one and going down the other side. And the last man on the top of the wall ready to go down into the graveyard was Brian Ó Braonacháin.

But a big blast of wind came and he was swept

off up into the sky. He was blown to the east and he was blown to the west. When he fell down to the ground, he could see neither the graveyard nor the coffin nor the funeral. But where did he fall? He fell down on the flagstone beside the well where he had been at the beginning of the night. He looked at the bucket and the water was hardly dry on the outside of it.

He took the bucket and up he went into the house. The old man and the old woman were sitting where he had left them at nightfall. He left the bucket by the dresser and he came up and sat between the pair of them again.

"Now, Brian," said the old man, "can you tell a fairy tale?"

"I can," said he, "I am the man who has got a story to tell."

He began to tell the old woman and the old man what he had gone through since nightfall.

"Well, Brian," said the old man, "wherever you are from now on, and whenever anybody asks you to tell a story, tell them that story, and you are the man who will have a story to tell."

The old woman got up and made Brian a good supper. When he had had his supper she made up a feather-bed for him and he went to bed and he wasn't in bed long before he fell asleep, for he was tired after all he had gone through since nightfall. When he woke in the morning, where was he? He was lying in Alt an Torr outside Barr an Gaoith with his head on two bundles of rods. He got up and went home and he never cut a rod from that day to this.

# Legends

# the Banshee

**t**he Reverend Charles Bunworth was rector of Buttevant, in the county Cork, about the middle of the last century. He was a man of unaffected piety, and of sound learning; pure in heart, and benevolent in intention. By the rich he was respected, and by the poor beloved, nor did a difference of creed prevent their looking up to "the minister" (so was Mr. Bunworth called by them) in matters of difficulty and in seasons of distress, confident of receiving from him the advice and assistance that a father would afford to his children. He was the friend and the benefactor of the surrounding country—to him, from the neighboring town of Newmarket, came both Curran and Yelverton for advice and instruction, previous to their entrance at Dublin college. Young, indigent, and inexperienced, these afterwards eminent men received from him, in addition to the advice they sought, pecuniary aid; and the brilliant career which was theirs justified the discrimination of the giver.

But what extended the fame of Mr. Bunworth far beyond the limits of the parishes adjacent to his own, was his performance on the Irish harp, and his hospitable reception and entertainment of the poor harpers who traveled from house to house about the country. Grateful to their patron, these itinerant minstrels sang his praises to the tingling accompaniment of their harps, invoking in return for his bounty abundant blessings on his white head, and celebrating in their rude verses the blooming charms of his daughters, Elizabeth and Mary. It was all these poor fellows could do; but who can doubt that their gratitude was sincere, when, at the time of Bunworth's death, no less than fifteen harps were deposited on the loft of his granary, bequeathed to him by the last members of a race which has now ceased to exist. Trifling, no doubt, in intrinsic value were the relics, yet there is something in gifts of the heart that merits preservation; and it is to be regretted that, when he died, these harps were broken up one after the other, and used as fire-wood by an ignorant follower of the family, who, on their removal to Cork for a temporary change of scene, was left in charge of the house.

The circumstances attending the death of Mr. Bunworth may be doubted by some; but there are still living credible witnesses who declare their authenticity, and who can be produced to attest most, if not all of the following particulars.

About a week previous to his dissolution, and early in the evening, a noise was heard at the hall-door resembling the shearing of sheep; but at the time no particular attention was paid to it. It was near eleven o'clock the same night, when Kavanagh, the herdsman, returned from Mallow, whither he had been sent in the afternoon for some medicine, and was observed by Miss Bunworth, to whom he delivered the parcel, to be much agitated. At this time, it must be observed, her father was by no means considered in danger.

"What is the matter, Kavanagh?" asked Miss Bunworth, but the poor fellow, with a bewildered look, only uttered, "The master, Miss—the master—he is going from us," and, overcome with real grief, he burst into a flood of tears.

Miss Bunworth, who was a woman of strong nerve, inquired if anything he had learned in Mallow induced him to suppose that her father was worse.

"No, Miss," said Kavanagh, "it was not in Mallow—"

"Kavanagh," said Miss Bunworth, with that stateliness of manner for which she is said to have been remarkable, "I fear you have been drinking, which I must say I did not expect at such a time as the present, when it was your duty to have kept yourself sober—I thought you might have been trusted—what should we have done if you had broken the medicine bottle, or lost it? For the doctor said it was of the greatest consequence that your master should take it tonight. But I shall speak to you in the morning, when you are in a fitter state to understand what I say."

Kavanagh looked up with a stupidity of aspect which did not serve to remove the impression of his being drunk, as his eyes appeared heavy and dull after the flood of tears—but his voice was not that of an intoxicated person.

"Miss," said he, "as I hope to receive mercy hereafter, neither bit nor sup has passed my lips since I left this house, but the master—"

"Speak softly," said Miss Bunworth, "he sleeps, and is going on as well as we could expect."

"Praise be to God for that, any way," replied Kavanagh, "but oh! miss, he is going from us surely—we will lose him—the master —we will lose him, we will lose him!" and he wrung his hands together.

"What is it you mean, Kavanagh?" asked Miss Bunworth.

"Is it mean?" said Kavanagh, "the Banshee

has come for him, Miss, and tis not I alone who have heard her."

"Tis an idle superstition," said Miss Bunworth.

"May be so," replied Kavanagh, as if the words "idle superstition" only sounded upon his ear without reaching his mind— "May be so," he continued, "but as I came through the glen of Ballybeg, she was along with me keening and screeching and clapping her hands, by my side every step of the way, with her long white hair falling all about her shoulders, and I could hear her repeat the master's name every now and then, as plain as ever I heard it. When I came to the old abbey, she parted from me there, and turned into the pigeon-field next the berrin ground, and folding her cloak about her, down she sat under the tree that was struck by the lightning, and began keening so bitterly, that it went through one's heart to hear it."

"Kavanagh," said Miss Bunworth, who had, however, listened attentively to this remarkable relation, "my father is, I believe, better, and I hope will himself soon be up and able to convince you that all this is but your own fancy; nevertheless, I charge you not to mention what you have told me, for there is no occasion to frighten your fellow-servants with the story."

Mr. Bunworth gradually declined, but nothing particular occurred until the night previous to his death. That night both his daughters, exhausted from continued attendance and watching, were prevailed upon to seek some repose, and an elderly lady, a near relative and friend of the family, remained by the bedside of their father. The old gentleman then lay in the parlor, where he had been in the morning removed at his own request, fancying the change would afford him relief, and the head of his bed was placed close to the window. In a room adjoining sat some male friends, and as usual on like occasions of illness, in the kitchen many of the followers of the family had assembled.

The night was serene and moonlight—the sick man slept—and nothing broke the stillness of their melancholy watch, when the little party in the room adjoining the parlor, the door of which stood open, was suddenly roused by a sound at the window near the bed: a rose-tree grew outside the window so close as to touch the glass, this was forced aside with some noise, and a low moaning was heard, accompanied by clapping of hands, as if of a female in deep affliction. It seemed as if the sound proceeded from a person holding her mouth close to the window. The lady who sat by the bedside of Mr. Bunworth went into the adjoining room, and in the tone of alarm, inquired of the gentlemen there if they heard the Banshee? Skeptical of supernatural appearances, two of them rose hastily and went out to discover the cause of these sounds, which they also had distinctly heard. They walked around the house, examining every spot of ground, particularly near the window from whence the voice had proceeded, but their search was in vain—they could perceive nothing, and an unbroken stillness reigned without. Yet hoping to dispel the mystery, they continued their search anxiously along the road, from the straightness of which and the lightness of the night, they were enabled to see some distance around them, but all was silent and deserted, and they returned surprised and disappointed. How much more then were they astonished at learning that the whole time of their absence, those who remained within the house had heard the moaning and clapping of hands even louder and more distinct than before they had gone out, and no sooner was the door of the room closed on them, than they again heard the same mournful sounds! Every succeeding hour the sick man became worse, and when the first glimpse of the morning appeared, Mr. Bunworth expired.

# the phooka
## or the spirit horse

The history of Morty Sullivan ought to be a warning to all young men to stay at home, and to live decently and soberly if they can, and not to go roving about the world. Morty, when he had just turned of fourteen, ran away from his father and mother, who were a mighty respectable old couple, and many and many a tear they shed on his account. It is said they both died broken-hearted for his loss: all they ever learned about him was that he went on board of a ship bound to America.

Thirty years after the old couple had been laid peacefully in their graves, there came a stranger to Beerhaven inquiring after them—it was their son, Morty; and to speak the truth of him, his heart did seem full of sorrow, when he heard that his parents were dead and gone—but what else could he expect to hear? Repentance generally comes when it is too late.

Morty Sullivan, however, as an atonement for his sins, was recommended to perform a pilgrimage to the blessed chapel of St. Gobnate, which is in a wild place called Ballyvourney.

This he readily undertook, and willing to lose no time, commenced his journey that afternoon. Morty had not proceeded many miles before the evening came on: there was no moon, and the starlight was obscured by a thick fog, which ascended from the valleys. His way was through a mountainous country, with many cross-paths and by-ways, so that it was difficult for a stranger like Morty to travel without a guide. He was anxious to reach his destination, and exerted himself to do so, but the fog grew thicker and thicker, and at last he became doubtful if the track he was on led to St. Gobnate's chapel. Seeing therefore a light which he imagined not to be far off, he went towards it, and when he thought himself close to it, the light suddenly seemed at a great distance, twinkling dimly through the fog. Though Morty felt some surprise at this, he was not disheartened, for he thought that it was a light that the blessed Saint Gobnate had sent to guide his feet through the mountains to her chapel.

Thus did he travel for many miles, continually, as he believed, approaching the light, which would suddenly start off to a great distance. At length he came so close as to perceive that the light came from a fire, seated beside which he plainly saw an old woman—then, indeed, his faith was a little shaken, and much did he wonder that both the fire and the old woman should travel before him, so many weary miles, and over such uneven roads.

"In the pious names of Saint Gobnate, and her preceptor Saint Abban," said Morty, "how can that burning fire move on so fast before me, and who can that old woman be sitting beside the moving fire?"

These words had no sooner passed Morty's lips than he found himself, without taking another step, close to this wonderful fire, beside which the old woman was sitting munching her supper. With every wag of the old woman's jaw her eyes would roll fiercely upon Morty, as if she was angry at being disturbed, and he saw with more astonishment than ever that her eyes were neither black, nor blue, nor gray, nor hazel, like the human eye, but of a wild red color, like the eye of a ferret. If before he wondered at the fire, much greater was his wonder at the old woman's appearance, and stout-hearted as he was, he could not but look upon her with fear— judging, and judging rightly, that it was for no good purpose her supping in so unfrequented a place, and at so late an hour, for it was near midnight. She said not one word, but munched, and munched away, while Morty looked at her in silence.—"What's your name?" at last demanded the old hag, a sulphureous puff coming out of her mouth, her nostrils distending, and her eyes growing redder than ever, when she had finished her question.

Plucking up all his courage, "Morty Sullivan," replied he, "at your service," meaning the latter words only in civility.

"Ubbubbo!" said the old woman, "we'll soon see that," and the red fire of her eyes turned into a pale green color. Bold and fearless as Morty was, yet much did he tremble at hearing this dreadful exclamation, he would have fallen down on his knees and prayed to Saint Gobnate, or any other saint, for he was not particular, but he was so petrified with horror, that he could not move in the slightest way, much less go down on his knees.

"Take hold of my hand, Morty," said the old woman. "I'll give you a horse to ride that will soon carry you to your journey's end." So saying, she led the way, the fire going before them, it is beyond mortal knowledge to say how, but on it went, shooting out bright tongues of flame, and flickering fiercely.

Presently they came to a natural cavern in the side of the mountain, and the old hag called aloud in a most discordant voice for her horse! In a moment a jet-black steed started from its gloomy stable, the rocky floor of which rung with a sepulchral echo to the clanging hoofs.

"Mount, Morty, mount!" cried she, seizing him with supernatural strength, and forcing him upon the back of the horse. Morty finding human power of no avail, muttered "Oh that I had spurs!" and tried to grasp the horse's mane, but he caught at a shadow, which nevertheless bore him up and bounded forward with him, now springing down a fearful precipice, now clearing the rugged bed of a torrent, and rushing like the dark midnight storm through the mountains.

The following morning Morty Sullivan was discovered by some pilgrims (who came that way after taking their rounds at Gougane Barra) lying on the flat of his back, under a steep cliff, down which he had been flung by the Phooka. Morty was severely bruised by the fall, and he is said to have sworn on the spot, by the hand of O'Sullivan (and that is no small oath), never again to take a full quart bottle of whiskey with him on a pilgrimage.

# Legend of knocksheogowna

In Tipperary is one of the most singularly shaped hills in the world. It has got a peak at the top like a conical nightcap thrown carelessly over your head as you awake in the morning. On the very point is built a sort of lodge, where in the summer the lady who built it and her friends used to go on parties of pleasure, but that was long after the days of the fairies, and it is, I believe, now deserted.

But before the lodge was built, or an acre sown, there was close to the head of the hill a large pasturage, where a herdsman spent his days and nights among the herd. The spot had been an old fairy ground, and the good people were angry that the scene of their light and airy gambols should be trampled by the rude hoofs of bulls and cows. The lowing of the cattle sounded sad in their ears, and the chief of the fairies of the hill determined in person to drive away the new comers, and the way she thought of was this. When the harvest nights came on, and the moon shone bright and brilliant over the hill, and the cattle were lying down hushed and quiet, and the herdsman wrapt in his mantle was musing with his heart gladdened by the glorious company of the stars twinkling above him, bathed in the flood of light bursting all over the sky, she would come and dance before him—now in one shape—now in another—but all ugly and frightful to behold. One time she would be a great horse, and with wings of an eagle, and a tail like a dragon, hissing loud and spitting fire. Then in a moment she would change into a little man lame of a leg, with a bull's head, and a lambent flame playing round it. Then into a great ape, with duck's feet and a turkeycock's tail. But I should be all day about it were I to tell you all the shapes she took. And then she would roar, or neigh, or hiss, or bellow, or howl, or hoot, as never yet was roaring, neighing, hissing, bellowing, howling, or hooting, heard in this world before or since. The poor herdsman would cover his face, and call on all saints for help, but it was no use. With one puff of her breath she would blow away the fold of his great coat, let him hold it never so tightly over his eyes, and not a saint in heaven paid him the slightest attention. And to make matters worse, he never could stir, no, nor even shut his eyes, but there was obliged to stay, held by what power he knew not, gazing at these terrible sights until the hair of his head would lift his hat half a foot over his crown, and his teeth would be ready to fall out from chattering. But the cattle would scamper about mad, as if they were bitten by the fly, and this would last until the sun rose over the hill.

The poor cattle from want of rest were pining away, and food did them no good, besides, they met with accidents without end. Never a night passed that some of them did not fall into a pit, and get maimed, or may be, killed. Some would tumble into a river and be drowned: in a word, there seemed never to be an end of the accidents. But what made the matter worse, there could not be a herdsman got to tend the cattle by night. One visit from the fairy would drive the stoutest-hearted almost mad. The owner of the ground did not know what to do. He offered double, treble, quadruple wages, but not a man could be found for the sake of money to go through the horror of facing the fairy. She rejoiced at the successful issue of her project, and continued her pranks. The herd gradually thinning, and no man daring to remain on the ground, the fairies came back in numbers and gamboled as merrily as before, quaffing dewdrops from acorns, and spreading their feast on the heads of capacious mushrooms.

What was to be done, the puzzled farmer thought in vain. He found that his substance was daily diminishing, his people terrified, and his rent-day coming round. It is no wonder that he looked gloomy, and walked mournfully down the road. Now in that part of the world dwelt a man of the name of Larry Hoolahan, who played on the pipes better than any other player within fifteen parishes. A roving dashing blade was Larry, and feared nothing. Give him plenty of liquor, and he would defy the devil. He would face a mad bull, or fight single-handed against a fairy. In one of his gloomy walks the farmer met him, and on Larry's asking the cause of his down looks, he told him all his misfortunes. "If that is all ails you," said Larry, "make your mind easy. Were there as many fairies on Knocksheogowna as there are potato blossoms in Eliogurty, I would face them. It would be a queer thing, indeed, if I, who never was afraid of a proper man, should turn my back upon a brat of a fairy not the bigness of one's thumb." "Larry," said the farmer, "do not talk so bold, for you know not who is hearing you, but if you make your words good, and watch my herds for a week on the top of the mountain, your hand shall be free of my dish till the sun has burnt itself down the bigness of a farthing rushlight."

The bargain was struck, and Larry went to the hill-top, when the moon began to peep over the brow. He had regaled at the farmer's house, and was bold with the extract of barleycorn. So he took his seat on a big stone under a hollow hill, with his back to the wind, and pulled out his pipes. He had not played long when the voice of the fairies was heard upon the blast, like a low stream of music. Presently they burst into a good laugh, and Larry could plainly hear one say, "What! another man upon the fairies' ring? Go to him, queen, and make him repent his rashness," and they flew away. Larry felt them pass by his face as they flew like a swarm of midges, and, looking up hastily, he saw between the moon and him a great black cat, standing on the very tip of its claws, with its back up, and mewing with a voice of a water-mill. Presently it swelled up towards the sky, and, turning round on its left hind leg, whirled till it fell on the ground, from which it started in the shape of a salmon, with a cravat round its neck, and a pair of new top boots. "Go on, jewel," said Larry, "if you dance, I'll pipe," and he struck up. So she turned into this, and that, and the other, but still Larry played on, as he well knew how. At last she lost patience, as ladies will do when you do not mind their scolding, and changed herself into a calf, milk-white as the cream of Cork, and with eyes as mild as those of the girl I love. She came up gentle and fawning, in hopes to throw him off his guard by quietness, and then to work him some wrong. But Larry was not deceived, for when she came up, he, dropping his pipes, leaped on her back.

Now from the top of Knocksheogowna, as you look westward to the broad Atlantic, you will see the Shannon, queen of rivers, "spreading like a sea," and running on in gentle course to mingle with the ocean through the fair city of Limerick. It on this night shone under the moon, and looked beautiful from the distant hill. Fifty boats were gliding up and down the street current, and the song of the fishermen rose gaily from the shore. Larry, as I said before, leaped upon the back of the fairy, and she, rejoiced at the opportunity, sprung from the hill-top, and bounded clear, at one jump, over the Shannon, flowing as it was just ten miles from the mountain's base. It was done in a second, and when she alighted on the distant bank, kicking up her heels, she flung Larry on the soft turf. No sooner was he thus planted, than he looked her straight in the face, and, scratching his head, cried out, "By my word, well done! that was not a bad leap for a calf!"

She looked at him for a moment, and then assumed her own shape. "Laurence," said she, "you are a bold fellow, will you come back the way you went?" "And that's what I will," said he, "if you let me." So changing to a calf again, again Larry got on her back, and at another bound they were again upon the top of Knocksheogowna. The fairy once more resuming her figure, addressed him: "You have shown so much courage, Laurence," said she, "that while you keep herds on this hill you never shall be molested by me or mine. The day dawns, go down to the farmer, and tell him this, and if any thing I can do may be of service to you, ask and you shall have it." She vanished accordingly, and kept her word in never visiting the hill during Larry's life: but he never troubled her with requests. He piped and drank at the farmer's expense, and roosted in his chimney corner, occasionally casting an eye to the flock. He died at last, and is buried in a green valley of pleasant Tipperary: but whether the fairies returned to the hill of Knocksheogowna after his death is more than I can say.

# the changeling

a young woman, whose name was Mary Scannell, lived with her husband not many years ago at Castle Martyr. One day in harvest time she went with several more to help in binding up the wheat, and left her child, which she was nursing, in a corner of the field, quite safe, as she thought, wrapped up in her cloak. When she had finished her work, she returned where the child was, but in place of her own child she found a thing in the cloak that was not half the size, and that kept up such a crying you might have heard it a mile off: so she guessed how the case was, and, without stop or stay, away she took it in her arms, pretending to be mighty fond of it all the while, to a wise woman, who told her in a whisper not to give it enough to eat, and to beat and pinch it without mercy, which Mary Scannell did, and just in one week after to the day, when she awoke in the morning, she found her own child lying by her side in the bed! The fairy that had been put in its place did not like the usage it got from Mary Scannell, who understood how to treat it, like a sensible woman as she was, and away it went after the week's trial, and sent her own child back to her.

# sayings

**a** man that can't laugh at himself should be given a mirror.

A man takes a drink; the drink takes a drink; the drink takes the man.

A narrow neck keeps the bottle from being emptied in one swig.

Morning is the time to pity the sober. The way they're feeling then is the best they're going to feel all day.

The devil invented Scotch whiskey to make Irish poor.

You can lead the horse to the well but you can't make him drink.

The last straw broke the horse's back.

Firelight will not let you read fine stories but it's warm and you won't see the dust on the floor.

If the head cannot bear the glory of the crown, better be without it.

Character is better than wealth.

In slender currents comes good luck; in rolling torrents comes misfortune.

Better the coldness of a friend than the sweetness of an enemy.

**B**etter to come in at the end of a feast than at the beginning of a fight.

Never let your right hand know what your left hand is doing.

It's as foolish to let a fool kiss you as it is to let a kiss fool you.

A friend's eye is the best mirror.

**B**e nice to them on the way up. You might meet them all on the way down.

If a man fools me once, shame on him. If he fools me twice, shame on me.

The tree remains, but not the hand that planted it.

Befriend who you wish but make sure you know what side your bread is buttered on.

There's no point in keeping a dog if you are going to do your own barking.

Better an ass that carries you than a fine horse that throws you.

Forsake not a friend of many years for the acquaintance of a day.

Let your anger set with the sun and not rise again with it.

# JOKES &
# LIMERICKS

Definition of an Irish husband:

He hasn't kissed his wife for twenty years but
he will kill any man who does.

Courtship is a time during which the girl
decides whether she can do better or not.

What do you call an Irishman who knows how to control a wife?

A bachelor.

Dinny was standing in the street the other day when an English chap came up to him and said,

"I say old chap, could you show me the way to the nearest boozer?"

Says Dinny, hopefully,

"You"re looking at him."

What do you find written on the bottom of Cork beer bottles?

Open other end.

What do you find written on the top of Cork beer bottles?

See other end for instructions.

What's the best thing that ever came out of Cork?

The road to Dublin.

# how do you make a Kerry cocktail?

Take a half glass of whiskey and add it to another half glass of whiskey.

To protect his precious pint on the bar counter while he goes to the buckets, a Dublin man scribbles a note and leaves it beside the glass:

"I have spit in this pint."

When he returns to his drink he notices an addition to his note which reads:

"So have I."

A lassie at Cahermee Fair,
Was having her first love affair.
  As she climbed into bed
  To the tinker she said:
"Do you mind if I start with a prayer?"

An Irishman owned an ould barge,
But his nose was exceedingly large.
  But in fishing by night
  It supported a light—
Which helped the old man with his charge.

A young lad from near South Donegal
  Who went to a Fancy Dress Ball
    Dressed up like a tree
    But he failed to foresee
His abuse by the dogs near the hall.

a lassie from Borriskane
Who went and undressed in a train,
   A saucy old porter,
   Saw more than he ought-er,
And asked her to do it again!

A woman who lived outside Cobh,
Got a notion to marry, by Jove,
   She nabbed a young sailor,
   Who swore he'd ne'er fail her.
Which ended his days on the rove!

A farmer from near Castlemaine
   Whose legs were cut off by a train.
      When his friends said: "How sad,"
      He replied: "I am glad.
   For I've lost my varicose vein."

There was a young lassie from Crosser,
Who in spiritual things was a messer.
   When sent to the priest,
   This lewd little beast,
Did her best to seduce her confessor.

A young lass from near Killenaule
   Wore a newspaper dress to a ball.
   The dress it caught fire
   Burnt up the entire—
Front page, sporting section and all!

An Irishman said with a grouch,
"Tis winter when you sneeze and you slouch,
   You can't take your women,
   In a canoe or swimming,
But a lot can be done on a couch!"